# American Museum of Natural History

## On the Trail of

# Incredible
# Dinosaurs

### William Lindsay

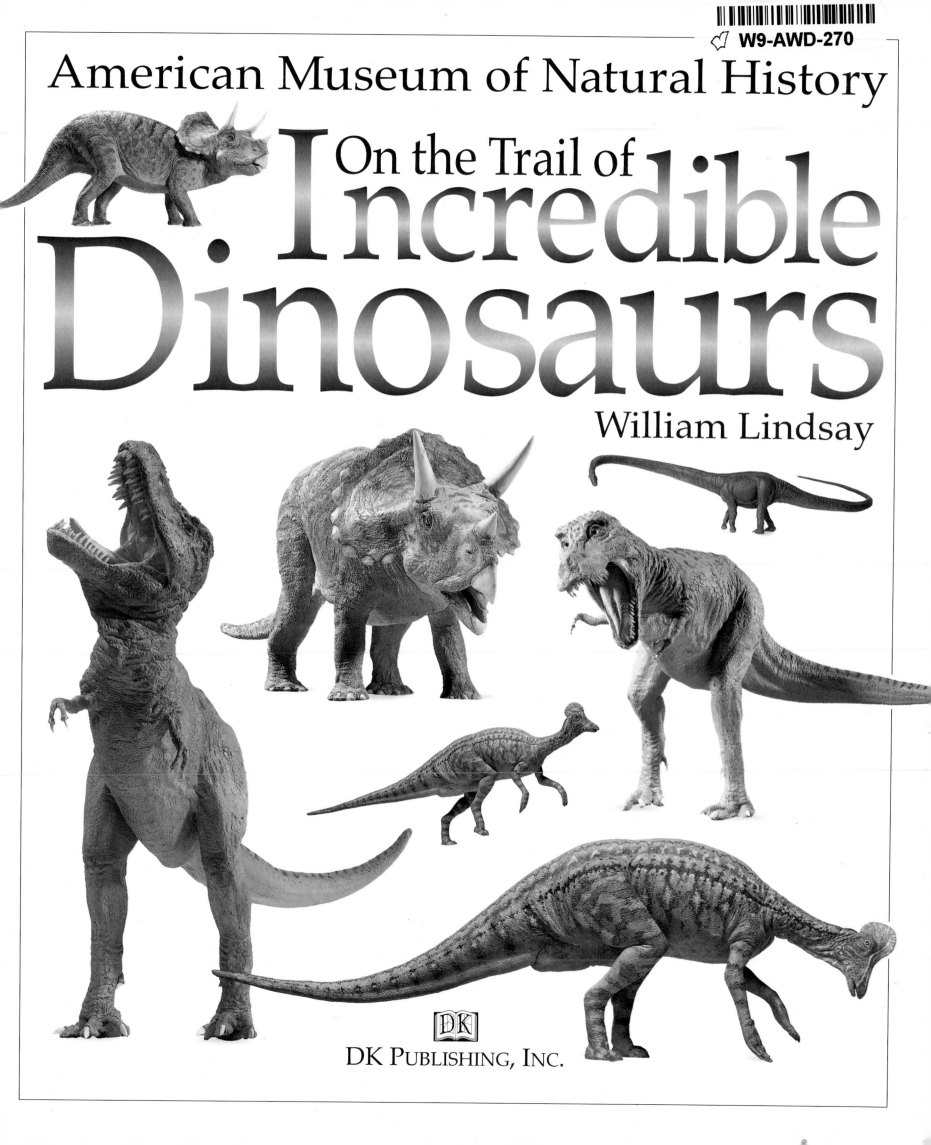

DK PUBLISHING, INC.

## A DK PUBLISHING BOOK

**Project editor** Monica Byles
**Art editors** Penny Lamprell and Peter Radcliffe
**Managing art editor** Chris Scollen
**Managing editor** Jane Yorke
**Production** Louise Barratt, Susannah Straughan, and Neil Palfreyman

**Research** Mary Ann Lynch
**Illustration** Simone Boni/L.R. Galante
**Dinosaur models** Graham High/Jeremy Hunt/Centaur Studios
**Model photography** Dave King
**Museum photography** Lynton Gardiner
**US Consultant** Dr. Mark Norell, The American Museum
of Natural History, New York
**UK consultant** Dr. Angela Milner, The Natural History Museum, London

First American Edition, 1998

2 4 6 8 10 9 7 5 3

Published in the United States by DK Publishing, Inc., 95 Madison Avenue, New York, NY 10016

Visit us on the World Wide Web at http://www.dk.com

Lindsay, William.
    On the trail of incredible dinosaurs / William Lindsay. – 1st American ed.
    p.    cm.
    At head of title: American Museum of Natural History.
    Includes index.
    Summary: Presents facts about four dinosaur species: tyrannosaurus rex, barosaurus, corythosaurus,
and triceratops.
    ISBN 0-7894-3628-0 (alk. paper)
    1. Dinosaurs–Juvenile literature.    1. [Dinosaurs.]    I. American Museum of Natural History.    II. Title.
QE862.D5L534 1998
567.9–DC21                                                                                      98–26396
                                                                                                      CIP
                                                                                                      AC

ISBN 0-7894-3628-0

Color reproduction by Colourscan, Singapore
Printed and bound in Italy by Graphicom

# CONTENTS

# INTRODUCTION

About 230 million years ago an extraordinary group of animals appeared on Earth – dinosaurs. Dinosaurs were reptiles. They had scaly skins and laid eggs that had tough, waterproof shells. They lived only on land; there were no swimming or flying dinosaurs. The earliest dinosaurs were small, two-legged meat-eaters, but they had something that gave them a distinct advantage over all the other reptiles – the ability to walk upright. Their legs were held directly beneath their bodies. This helped to support their body weight and balance their head and tail-ends. All other reptiles had legs that stuck out sideways. The dinosaurs' straight legs and balanced body meant that they could run fast on just their back legs and use their front limbs to feed, or for attack and defense. Those that were really large could support their weight on all four legs and still move easily. Scientists think that the main reason why dinosaurs became so successful was their ability to walk upright. These amazing creatures soon came to dominate life on land and remained supreme for more than 150 million years until their dramatic disappearance – an extinction that remains a mystery to this day. However, by studying the fossilized remains of dinosaurs, scientists have been able to piece together a great deal about the past lives of these incredible animals.

This book takes you on a journey of discovery into the lost worlds of four great dinosaurs: *Tyrannosaurus rex*, *Barosaurus*, *Corythosaurus*, and *Triceratops*. You will find out how complete skeletons of these dinosaurs were found, excavated, and pieced together. Then you will discover how these creatures lived. Use the glossary and pronunciation guide on pages 92 and 93 to help you with unfamiliar words.

**Dr. Mark Norell**
**Chairman and Associate Curator**
**Department of Vertebrate Paleontology**
**American Museum of Natural History, New York City**

NOTE: IN THIS BOOK WE HAVE SOMETIMES USED "*TYRANNOSAURUS REX*" (THE FULL, TWO-WORD SCIENTIFIC NAME FOR THIS DINOSAUR) BECAUSE IT IS WIDELY KNOWN. FOR THE OTHER THREE DINOSAURS WE HAVE USED THE FIRST PART OF THEIR NAMES ONLY. THEIR FULL SPECIES NAMES ARE AS FOLLOWS: THERE ARE TWO SPECIES OF *BAROSAURUS* – *BAROSAURUS LENTUS* AND *BAROSAURUS AFRICANUS*; *CORYTHOSAURUS*' FULL SCIENTIFIC NAME IS *CORYTHOSAURUS CASUARIUS*; *TRICERATOPS*' FULL SCIENTIFIC NAME IS *TRICERATOPS HORRIDUS*.

# TYRANNOSAURUS REX

*Tyrannosaurus rex* lived in western North America between 67 and 65 million years ago. It was one of the largest meat-eating animals that has ever lived on land, and one of the last dinosaurs to walk the Earth.

Fossil remains of *Tyrannosaurus rex* are rare. Apart from single teeth, fewer than twenty fossil specimens have been found, and only five or six of these are reasonably complete skeletons. One of the best finds of all, collected in 1908 by the famous American dinosaur hunter Barnum Brown, features in this book.

How do we know so much about *Tyrannosaurus rex* from so few remains? Careful study of its bones and teeth provides information about *Tyrannosaurus rex's* lifestyle and its place in evolution. We now know that it was not related to other large meat-eating dinosaurs but to advanced small meat-eaters like *Deinonychus* and *Troodon*, and that its closest living relatives are the birds. We also know what other kinds of dinosaurs shared its world.

However, the remains of *Tyrannosaurus rex* will never reveal what the living animal was really like. Paleontologists can only make educated guesses as to how it behaved, how fast it ran, and the color of its skin. Facts such as these remain a mystery, lost forever in the past.

# TYRANT LIZARD

*T*yrannosaurus rex is one of the most famous of all the dinosaurs. Even its name makes you imagine huge, nightmarish monsters. But *Tyrannosaurus* was no make-believe monster. Millions of years after its death, scientists are now able to piece together this great creature from its fossilized remains, providing some answers to many puzzling questions.

## Scaly skin
Rare impressions of dinosaur skin have been found fossilized in ancient rocks. It was thick, tough, scaly, and waterproof, similar to that of modern-day reptiles, like the crocodile.

*Tyrannosaurus rex*
(Tie-ran-oh-saw-rus recks) means "king of the tyrant lizard."
*Tyrannosaurus* means "tyrant lizard."

## Two types of dinosaur
Dinosaurs are divided into two groups by the shape and position of their hip or pelvic bones. "Bird-hipped" or ornithischian dinosaurs were plant-eaters; their two lower hip bones pointed backwards and down to accommodate their large guts. "Lizard-hipped" or saurischian dinosaurs, such as *Tyrannosaurus rex,* were primarily meat-eaters and had shorter, less bulky guts, allowing their hip bones to sit closer together. One of their two lower hip bones pointed forwards and their other bone pointed backwards.

*Heterodontosaurus*
"bird-hipped" dinosaur

*Struthiomimus*
"lizard-hipped" dinosaur

## Walking tall
Unlike most reptiles, whose legs sprawl out at the sides of their bodies, dinosaurs stood on legs held straight beneath their bodies. This enabled dinosaurs to move about more easily than other reptiles. Some dinosaurs walked on four legs. Others, such as *Tyrannosaurus rex,* walked on two.

## Meat-eater

Carnivores (meat-eaters) such as *Tyrannosaurus rex* had sharp teeth and claws for slicing into flesh. *Tyrannosaurus rex* had extremely strong jaws that were powered by mighty muscles, enabling it to open its mouth so wide that it could have swallowed a human in just two bites!

## FACT FILE

- **Lived:** 67-65 million years ago, during the late Cretaceous Period.

- **Family:** Tyrannosaurids, one of coelurosaurian group

- **Dinosaur type:** Lizard-hipped (saurischian)

- **Maximum life span:** Possibly up to 100 years

- **Diet:** Meat of dinosaurs and other animals

- **Weight when alive:** A little over 6 tons (up to 7 tonnes)

- **Height:** 18 ft (6m)

- **Length:** 42 ft (14 m)

- **Top speed:** Possibly up to 15 mph (25 km/h)

Like most two-legged predators, *Tyrannosaurus rex* could move quickly. However, *Tyrannosaurus* could probably not run at speed for long distances because of its great size.

## Lost worlds

Dinosaur species appeared and died out over three periods of the Earth's history. *Tyrannosaurus* lived at the end of the Cretaceous Period.

**TRIASSIC PERIOD**
248–205 million years ago

**JURASSIC PERIOD**
205–144 million years ago

**CRETACEOUS PERIOD**
144–65 million years ago

# FOSSIL FINDS

The story of the death, fossilization, and discovery of one *Tyrannosaurus rex* spans more than 65 million years. When *Tyrannosaurus* died at the end of the Cretaceous Period, it was buried under sand and mud, where its skeleton was slowly fossilized.

In July 1908, Barnum Brown, one of America's greatest dinosaur hunters, spotted the exposed *Tyrannosaurus* fossil bones jutting out of rocks near Hell Creek, Montana. Eight years earlier, Brown had discovered the first unfamiliar remains of this new dinosaur species, later named *Tyrannosaurus rex*. But the second find was much more complete. This 1908 specimen is still used to identify new *Tyrannosaurus* fossil specimens today.

**Journey through the earth**
After its death around 65 million years ago, the body of this *Tyrannosaurus rex* was not destroyed by other animals. The skeleton survived intact in its rocky grave for millions of years, until earth movements and weathering exposed it once more.

**Dry season**
A long drought has dried up the lush swamps and forests. A few plants still grow along old riverbeds.

**Wet season**
Later in the year, heavy rains bring flash floods. Dead animals and plants are buried in sand and mud as the waters subside.

**New life**
Hundreds of years later, the river has changed course. Other dinosaurs now feed on the plants that grow by the river.

**1 Alive and well**
*Tyrannosaurus* prowls along drying riverbeds, where other dinosaurs gather to feed and drink.

**2 Washed away**
Killed by disease, attack, or drowning, *Tyrannosaurus* is carried off in floodwaters.

**3 Dead and buried**
Buried under sand and mud, only bones and teeth remain. The dinosaur's soft flesh has long since rotted away.

**4 Turned to stone**
The skeleton is now buried under many layers of rock. Chemicals have slowly changed the bones into hard fossils.

**Terrible tooth**
Dinosaur teeth are often well-preserved as fossils, because they are hard and resistant to decay. A *Tyrannosaurus* tooth may be as long as 7 in (18 cm), with a sharp, serrated edge for cutting and tearing the flesh of its prey.

**5 Inside the Earth**
Movements deep below the Earth's crust force the *Tyrannosaurus* skeleton closer to the surface. The fossil bones are now cracked and broken.

## In the footsteps of Barnum Brown

The rocks of Hell Creek, Montana, were formed in the Late Cretaceous Period of the Earth's history. They belong to the time of the last dinosaurs and today are scoured for treasures by fossil hunters.

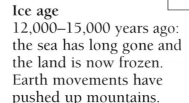

Hell Creek, Montana

Discovery site of *Tyrannosaurus rex*

## DINOSAUR DETECTIVE

### Barnum Brown (1873 – 1963)

Barnum Brown joined the American Museum of Natural History (AMNH) in New York in 1897. Nicknamed "Mr. Bones," Brown worked on the museum staff for 45 years. His skill in discovering fossils helped to give the AMNH the finest dinosaur collection in the world.

1873   Born in Carbondale, Kansas.
1895   Discovered a **Triceratops** skull in Wyoming.
1897   Joined AMNH as a paleontologist, at age of 24.
1900   Discovered the first fossils of **Tyrannosaurus rex**.
1908   Found the second **Tyrannosaurus rex** specimen.
1934   Made his greatest discovery of over 20 dinosaur skeletons at Howe Quarry, Wyoming.
1963   Died one week before his 90th birthday in New York.

### Dinosaur diggers
*Barnum Brown (center, front row) with his field team on one of many dinosaur field trips.*

## Seascape
Millions of years later, the dinosaurs have died out. The land where they once lived is now covered by sea.

## Ice age
12,000–15,000 years ago: the sea has long gone and the land is now frozen. Earth movements have pushed up mountains.

## 6 Into daylight
The rock of the ancient riverbed has been carved by wind and rain into hills and canyons. Weathering has finally brought the *Tyrannosaurus* fossils back to the surface.

# DIGGING FOR DINOSAURS

Like many dinosaur discoveries, the *Tyrannosaurus rex* specimen of 1908 was found in desolate, open country, far from the nearest settlement. Barnum Brown and his field team set up camp in the badlands of Montana, five days' travel by horsedrawn wagon from the nearest railway.

The excavation took three months of backbreaking work. Some of the *Tyrannosaurus* bones were easily removed from sand, but others were buried in rock as hard as granite. Scrapers, picks, shovels, and even dynamite were used to free the fossil bones.

Plaster jacket containing fossil

**Materials needed to make a plaster jacket**

Chisels for chipping rock

Burlap

**1 Excavating the fossils**
Once rubble had been cleared from around the skeleton, the fossil hunters carefully began to chip rock away from the individual bones. When the fragile fossils were exposed, they were then strengthened with glue and wrapped in burlap soaked in plaster of Paris.

**2 Shipping the fossils**
Once the protective plaster jacket had dried, each fossil could be removed from site. The fossils were hoisted into wooden crates. Each heavy crate was hauled by horse and cart to the railway, some 150 miles (240 km) away from the excavation site.

Missing or fragile bones, like those of the skull, were modeled in plaster.

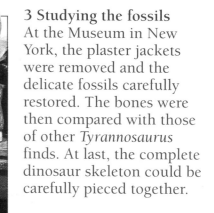

**3 Studying the fossils**
At the Museum in New York, the plaster jackets were removed and the delicate fossils carefully restored. The bones were then compared with those of other *Tyrannosaurus* finds. At last, the complete dinosaur skeleton could be carefully pieced together.

**4 Skeleton display**
In 1915, the scientists began to prepare the original fossils for a new museum display. Ropes and pulleys held all the heavy bones in place while the mount was built.

Trowel for mixing plaster

A lighter plaster cast was hung in place of the fragile, heavy skull.

Ropes held all the bones securely in position, while the supporting metal framework was built around the fossil skeleton.

The dinosaur builders worked from wooden platforms, laid across scaffolding, high above the Museum floor.

**Mini-dinosaurs**
The dinosaur builders made detailed scale models, one-sixth of life size, showing every bone in the skeleton of *Tyrannosaurus rex*. These models helped the scientists to experiment with different display positions for their fullsize mount. The model shown here demonstrates how *Tyrannosaurus rex* might have been mounted, gnawing on a carcass.

# RECONSTRUCTING TYRANNOSAURUS

The *Tyrannosaurus rex* skeleton found by Barnum Brown was put on display at the American Museum of Natural History in 1915, seven years after its discovery. The new mount was over 42 ft (14 m) long and stood nearly 18 ft (over 5 m) tall. *Tyrannosaurus* is easily recognized by its large skull and rib cage, long legs and tail, and by its strange, small arms. Scientists have puzzled over how the dinosaur might have used its arms. They probably would not have been helpful for feeding because they were too short to reach its mouth!

Correct position with tail held up off the ground

**Corrected reconstruction**
Carnosaurs, the family of large meat-eating dinosaurs like *Tyrannosaurus rex*, walked on two legs, not four. However, when the *Tyrannosaurus* skeleton was first reconstructed, it was shown with its tail resting on the ground and its body held upright. Scientists now believe that the living dinosaur held its body almost level with the ground, balanced by its tail held in the air.

**Towering monster**
If *Tyrannosaurus* were alive today, it would tower above most living land animals, including people.

Long jaws lined with meat-slicing, serrated teeth

**Front view**
Seen from the front, 65 million years after its death, *Tyrannosaurus rex* is still a terrifying example of the carnivorous dinosaurs.

Tiny arms have two clawed fingers on each hand.

The rib cage is deep at the front, but narrows toward the rear. The ribs curve inward to protect the soft organs in the body cavity.

Tail vertebrae

Bones of the feet were locked together for strength.

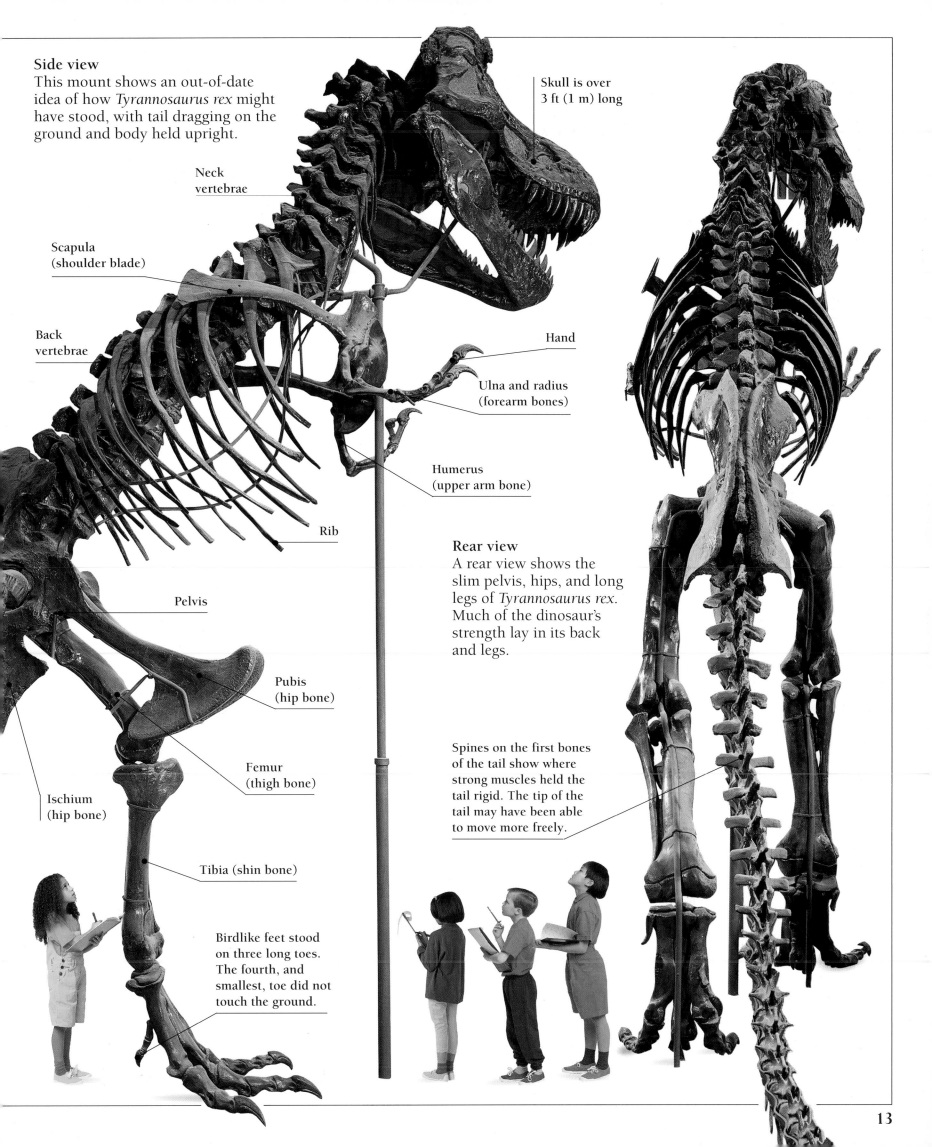

**Side view**
This mount shows an out-of-date idea of how *Tyrannosaurus rex* might have stood, with tail dragging on the ground and body held upright.

Skull is over 3 ft (1 m) long

Neck vertebrae

Scapula (shoulder blade)

Back vertebrae

Hand

Ulna and radius (forearm bones)

Humerus (upper arm bone)

Rib

**Rear view**
A rear view shows the slim pelvis, hips, and long legs of *Tyrannosaurus rex*. Much of the dinosaur's strength lay in its back and legs.

Pelvis

Pubis (hip bone)

Ischium (hip bone)

Femur (thigh bone)

Spines on the first bones of the tail show where strong muscles held the tail rigid. The tip of the tail may have been able to move more freely.

Tibia (shin bone)

Birdlike feet stood on three long toes. The fourth, and smallest, toe did not touch the ground.

# MUSCLE POWER

Tyrannosaurus rex needed powerful muscles to operate its enormous body. Muscles work by pulling on the parts of the bony skeleton to which they are attached, enabling limbs to bend or the tail to move. Because muscles are soft flesh and rot quickly, they do not fossilize.

Scientists can, however, reconstruct the shape, position, and size of dinosaur muscles by studying marks left on fossil bones, where the muscles once attached, and by studying birds. The findings are then compared with the muscle arrangement of modern-day animals. Scientists know, for instance, that muscles attached to the pelvis of *Tyrannosaurus* moved the large leg bones, while muscles attached to the neck vertebrae helped to move the creature's head.

**Strong muscles attaching the pelvis to the femur gave power for running.**

**One end of the femur joined the pelvis, while the other end formed part of the knee. Muscles helped to connect the bones, bend the knee, and turn the leg at the hip joint.**

**Inside the leg**
This model, made for museum display, shows the bones and muscles in the leg of *Albertosaurus*, a relative of *Tyrannosaurus rex*.

**Muscles connected the tibia and fibula with the knee and ankle.**

**Red muscle, rich in blood vessels**

**Smooth outer lining protecting muscle**

**Strong muscles around the ankle bones helped to power movement in the foot.**

*Albertosaurus*
*Albertosaurus* was a smaller relative of *Tyrannosaurus rex*. Like *Tyrannosaurus*, it was a fierce hunter with large, powerful legs. These two dinosaurs had a similar muscle structure.

**Long bones in the foot were fused together for added strength.**

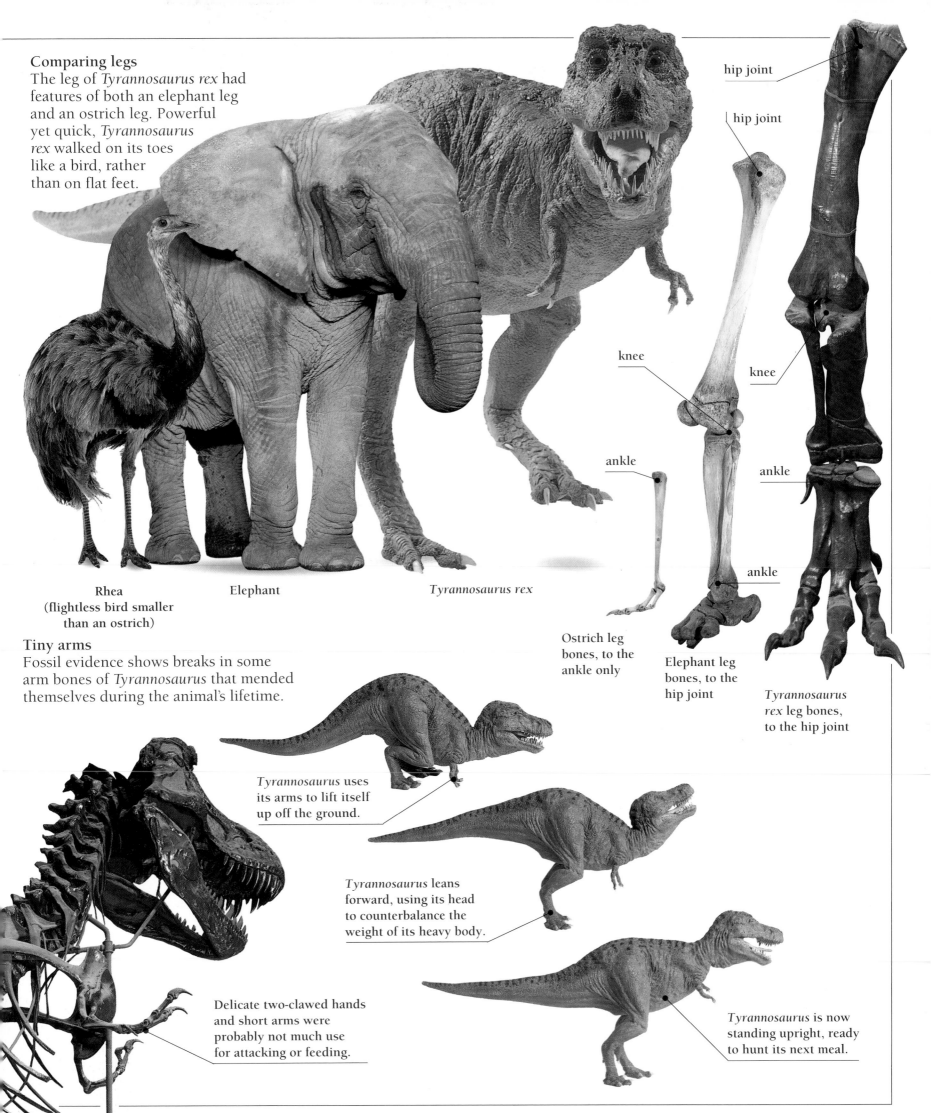

**Comparing legs**
The leg of *Tyrannosaurus rex* had features of both an elephant leg and an ostrich leg. Powerful yet quick, *Tyrannosaurus rex* walked on its toes like a bird, rather than on flat feet.

hip joint

hip joint

knee

knee

ankle

ankle

ankle

Rhea
(flightless bird smaller than an ostrich)

Elephant

*Tyrannosaurus rex*

Ostrich leg bones, to the ankle only

Elephant leg bones, to the hip joint

*Tyrannosaurus rex* leg bones, to the hip joint

**Tiny arms**
Fossil evidence shows breaks in some arm bones of *Tyrannosaurus* that mended themselves during the animal's lifetime.

*Tyrannosaurus* uses its arms to lift itself up off the ground.

*Tyrannosaurus* leans forward, using its head to counterbalance the weight of its heavy body.

Delicate two-clawed hands and short arms were probably not much use for attacking or feeding.

*Tyrannosaurus* is now standing upright, ready to hunt its next meal.

15

# MONSTER IN MOTION

Tyrannosaurus rex was a ferocious hunter of dinosaurs and other animals. It had a massive head and a sturdy neck that could deliver a deadly and crushing blow to its prey. Tyrannosaurus used its strong toes and sharp claws to hold down its victims, while its vicious teeth sliced into their flesh. Few animals could escape a Tyrannosaurus on the attack.

**Speeding dinosaur**
Some scientists believe that a charging Tyrannosaurus could reach a top speed of over 15 mph (25 km/h). Other experts claim it was capable of running at up to 40 mph (64 km/h), as fast as a modern white rhino.

**3 Spotting prey**
Tyrannosaurus sights a young dinosaur, grazing apart from its herd. Tyrannosaurus turns its head for a better view.

*Tyrannosaurus rex* had strong legs tucked under its bulky body, which supported its 6 ton (7 tonne) weight.

**2 On the prowl**
Tyrannosaurus moves forward, swinging powerful legs under its huge body.

**8 Deadly bite**
The knife-sharp fangs of Tyrannosaurus rex close in on its next meal. One swift bite to the neck slices through blood vessels and windpipe and crushes bone.

**1 Hungry hunter**
A hungry Tyrannosaurus hunts for a likely victim. Its keen senses are ready to detect the presence of another predator that might steal its kill.

As it moved along, *Tyrannosaurus* used its long tail to counterbalance the weight of its massive body.

**5 On the attack**
Now in full attack, *Tyrannosaurus* charges forward toward its prey.

**4 Ready to strike**
Sweeping its muscular tail around, *Tyrannosaurus* moves in for the kill. If its strike is unsuccessful, *Tyrannosaurus* will have wasted vital energy and alerted the herd of grazing dinosaurs to danger.

**7 In for the kill**
*Tyrannosaurus* lunges forward with open jaws to catch its prey.

**6 Towering tyrant**
*Tyrannosaurus* throws up its head and roars. Rearing overhead, *Tyrannosaurus* is a terrifying sight to its victim.

# GIANT JAWS

*T*yrannosaurus rex had one of the biggest and strongest heads of all the dinosaurs. This ferocious meat-eater could kill its prey with one crushing bite of its giant saber-toothed jaws, and then a twist of its powerful neck could tear away the first mouthful of meat. Even the tough, bony plates that shielded plant-eating dinosaurs of the time would have been savaged by *Tyrannosaurus'* immensely strong jaws and daggerlike fangs. Like other meat-eating dinosaurs, *Tyrannosaurus* was able to grow new teeth to replace those that were broken or worn down.

**Skull discovery**
The *Tyrannosaurus* skull shown here, found by Barnum Brown in Hell Creek, Montana, in 1908, is over 3 ft (1 m) long. Features such as the massive skull and jaw bones made it possible for *Tyrannosaurus* to swallow smaller dinosaurs whole.

A front view of the skull shows the huge bones, slightly crushed by fossilization.

Openings for the air passages to the nostril

Scientists have left some of the rock between the bones to support the shape of the heavy skull.

The giant, serrated teeth curve backward, designed to grip and rip apart carcasses. The teeth form a deep cutting edge as they increase in size from the front to the middle of the jaws.

New teeth grew to replace those that were old and worn.

Fine holes along the margin of the jaws show where blood vessels passed out of the bone to the skin.

The deep, strong lower jaw had a large area of bone where the jaw muscles attached.

**Bone-crusher**
*Tyrannosaurus rex* had enormous and powerful jaws, operated by thick masses of muscle. Other dinosaurs could make their mouths larger by flexing their skull bones at special joints, just as some reptiles do today.

Small bony crest
on the roof of
the skull

Eye socket

Muscles from the neck
connected to the wide
area of bone at the
back of the skull.

Spaces between the
skull bones made the
head lighter and left
room for muscles.

**Powerful neck**
Strong neck muscles supported
*Tyrannosaurus'* mighty skull.
*Tyrannosaurus* could move
its head in all directions,
which helped it hold
down struggling prey.

*Tyrannosaurus rex* may have
had better-positioned eyes for
hunting than other dinosaurs.
Forward-facing eyes helped
it keep its prey in sight
as it charged.

Skin covering a
special area of skull
at the side of the
animal's head formed
*Tyrannosaurus'* ear.

Its thick, large
tongue helped
*Tyrannosaurus*
process its food
before swallowing.

# KILLER INSTINCT

Tyrannosaurus rex was an animal well adapted for hunting. Bigger than any of the other meat-eating dinosaurs of its time, a 7 ton (8 tonne) *Tyrannosaurus* was powerful enough to attack even a 6 ton (6 tonne) heavily armored *Triceratops*. Its giant size was matched by an enormous appetite, and *Tyrannosaurus* seized every opportunity for catching a passing meal – the bigger the kill, the less hunting it had to do.

*Tyrannosaurus* was equipped with excellent tools for hunting and killing. In addition to the dinosaur's great size, strength, and fearsome teeth, it probably had good senses for seeing, hearing, and smelling its prey.

### Staying alive
Like all animals, *Tyrannosaurus rex* had to eat to live. Although it may have stolen kills made by smaller carnivores, *Tyrannosaurus* was better equipped than most to hunt its own prey.

Some worn *Tyrannosaurus rex* teeth suggest that the dinosaur was capable of biting through soft flesh to the hard bone.

### 1 Finding a meal
*Tyrannosaurus rex* has killed its prey and must devour it quickly, before it is stolen by other carnivores.

*Tyrannosaurus rex* may have needed to eat its own weight in meat every week.

### 2 Tearing flesh
*Tyrannosaurus* holds down the carcass with its clawed feet and rips off chunks of meat with its jaws. The dinosaur swallows its meal without chewing.

## Focusing on prey

Many dinosaurs had eyes at the sides of their head and saw a different view from each eye. Some animals, such as humans, have eyes that face forward and can form a single view. This lets them judge distances accurately.

*Tyrannosaurus rex* may have had eyes that faced forward, which helped it spot prey. No one knows if *Tyrannosaurus* saw in tones of gray or in color.

Single view from forward-facing eyes in color and in black and white

Double view from sideways-facing eyes in color and in black and white

Birdlike feet pinned the carcass to the ground.

Teeth were curved and serrated, designed to slice huge chunks of meat from the carcass.

## 3 Facing the competition

A second hungry *Tyrannosaurus* approaches, desperate to share in the kill. *Tyrannosaurus* prepares to defend its meal, and roars in an effort to frighten away its rival.

# FEROCIOUS FIGHTER

Tyrannosaurus rex was the top predator living in North America in the Late Cretaceous period. Like lions today, Tyrannosaurus preyed on the plant-eating animals in its area. But unlike lions, which hunt in packs, Tyrannosaurus rex probably hunted alone.

Skeletons of large carnivores like Tyrannosaurus rex are usually found singly, not in groups. In one part of Canada, only five out of 100 dinosaur finds have been large meat-eaters. Tyrannosaurus may have needed to eat a lot of dinosaur meat to satisfy its huge appetite.

**Face to face**
Although most animals will try to avoid a fight, they may attack one another over food. Few dinosaurs would have risked attacking Tyrannosaurus rex. One Tyrannosaurus skull with damaged bones suggests, however, that another Tyrannosaurus might have tried, perhaps to steal a kill.

A face-to-face struggle between two hungry Tyrannosaurus would have been one of the most fearsome battles ever.

**Gaping jaws**
The tooth-lined jaws of Tyrannosaurus rex were its main weapons. Its mouth and fierce roar might have scared another animal off without a fight.

**Deadly dance**
Tyrannosaurus challenges, shifting and dodging to show off its strength and size. This display may frighten the rival away.

**Ready to charge**
The massive, muscular legs are ready to carry Tyrannosaurus in a headlong charge at its enemy, if it finally has to fight for its meal.

**Cretaceous hunting ground**
*Tyrannosaurus* would have preyed on many species of dinosaur. Most would have kept their distance from such a ferocious predator.

*Ornithomimus*

*Parasaurolophus*

*Saurolophus*

**Safety in numbers**
*Triceratops*, one of the most common dinosaurs of the period, grazed in herds for protection.

*Edmontosaurus*

*Ankylosaurus*

**Fast runners**
Duck-billed dinosaurs, like *Saurolophus*, *Edmontosaurus*, and *Parasaurolophus*, as well as the fast-running *Ornithomimus*, feed nervously as the fight continues. At the first sign of danger, they will escape into the safety of the forest.

**Armored defense**
An armored *Ankylosaurus* backs away from battle. Even with its powerful, muscular tail club, the animal prefers to avoid any danger.

**Safe in the river**
River turtles have picked clean the carcass of a dead dinosaur. Swept there by last season's floodwaters, the skeleton is now left half-buried in the silted shallows of the stream.

**Swinging tails**
Tails raised for balance, the two dinosaurs shift position to catch one another off guard.

# TYRANNOSAURUS SPECIMEN AND FAMILY FACTS

- **Specimen number**: AMNH 5027
- **Excavated by**: Barnum Brown
- **Excavation**: 1908, at Hell Creek, Montana
- **Bones found**: Almost complete skeleton; missing the forelimbs and some leg bones which were modeled in plaster

- **Where displayed**: American Museum of Natural History, New York City*
- **First constructed**: 1915; made up primarily from original fossil bones; ropes and pulleys used during construction to hold all heavy bones in place

---

# 🏛 ON THE MUSEUM TRAIL 🏛

## A museum guide to tyrannosaur specimens
### A partial listing of both fossils and replica casts of fossils.

UNITED STATES
(*Tyrannosaurus*) University of Michigan Exhibit Museum, Ann Arbor, Michigan
(*Tyrannosaurus*) University of California, Museum of Paleontology, Berkeley, California
(*Tyrannosaurus*) Museum of the Rockies, Bozemann, Montana
(*Albertosaurus*) Field Museum of Natural History, Chicago, Illinois
(*Nanotyrannus*) Natural History Museum, Cleveland, Ohio
(*Tyrannosaurus*) Denver Museum of Natural History, Denver, Colorado
(*Tyrannosaurus*) The Museum, Michigan State University, East Lansing, Michigan

Carnosaur specimens may also be found in museums in Australia, Canada, France, Germany, Japan, Mongolia, Poland, Russia, Spain, Sweden, and the United Kingdom.

**Dinosaur display**
This is the specimen found by Brown in 1908. It was the first *Tyrannosaurus* skeleton ever built. It towered over other dinosaurs in the halls of the AMNH for many years.

(*Tyrannosaurus*)
   Los Angeles County Museum
   of Natural History,
   Los Angeles, California
(*Albertosaurus, Tyrannosaurus*)
   American Museum of Natural History,
   New York, New York
(*Tyrannosaurus*) Carnegie Museum of
   Natural History, Pittsburgh, Pennsylvania
(*Albertosaurus, Tyrannosaurus*) National Museum
   of Natural History, Smithsonian Institution,

*Tyrannosaurus rex* lived about 65 million years ago, at the end of the Cretaceous Period. It was one of the last dinosaurs.

*AMNH 5027 was completely remounted in a new pose for the revised AMNH dinosaur gallery opened in 1996.

**Tyrannosaurus relatives**
Tyrannosaurus and its fellow tyrannosaurids, *Albertosaurus* and *Tarbosaurus*, belong to a group of advanced meat-eaters called coelurosaurs. They are in turn related to *Allosaurus*, a tetanuran, and to ceratosaurs, such as *Ceratosaurus* and *Dilophosaurus*, which were a group of large early meat-eaters. All of these groups together form part of the larger group of theropods.

*Ceratosaurus* lived 150 million years ago in the Jurassic Period. It was less than half the size of *Tyrannosaurus rex*.

*Albertosaurus* was smaller than *Tyrannosaurus rex*. It lived in the Cretaceous Period and has been found in North America.

*Dilophosaurus* lived 200 million years ago, in the Early Jurassic Period. It was less than half the size of *Tyrannosaurus*.

*Tarbosaurus* was very similar to *Tyrannosaurus rex* but slightly smaller. Its remains have been found in Mongolia.

*Allosaurus* was a common hunter of 150 million years ago, in the Jurassic Period. Its fossils have been found in North America.

**Worlds apart**
Dinosaur remains have been found on every continent. New species of dinosaurs evolved and adapted over millions of years as climates and landscapes changed. This map shows areas where *Tyrannosaurus* and other theropods have been found.

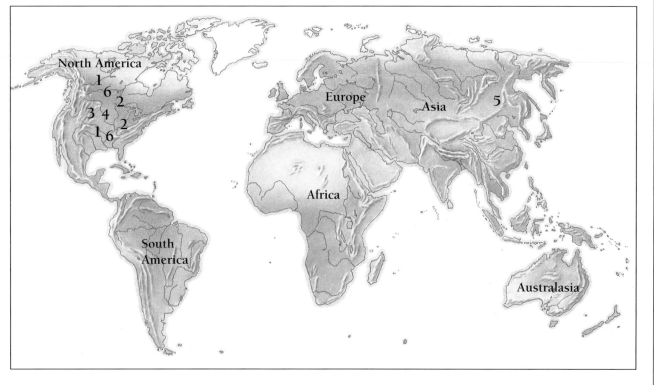

Key to map

1  *Albertosaurus*
2  *Allosaurus*
3  *Ceratosaurus*
4  *Dilophosaurus*
5  *Tarbosaurus*
6  *Tyrannosaurus*

North America

Europe

Asia

Africa

South America

Australasia

# BAROSAURUS

*Barosaurus* was one of the largest animals that has ever lived on land. This enormous creature, together with similar long-necked, four-footed dinosaurs, was the top plant-eater of its day, around 150 to 140 million years ago.

It is difficult for us today to imagine these gigantic animals wandering across the landscape. *Barosaurus* and its relatives were many times larger than the biggest land animal living today, the African elephant. But like the African elephant, *Barosaurus* was a social animal and probably lived in herds or family groups. Footprints and trackways of *Barosaurus* and its relatives provide us with vital clues to the everyday lives of these dinosaurs. We can see from 150-million-year-old trails left along a muddy riverbank in North America that a herd of these magnificent animals walked along, with the young animals following in the adults' footsteps.

The *Barosaurus* you will read about in this book is displayed at the American Museum of Natural History in New York City. It has been mounted rearing up on its hind legs to protect its baby from an attacking *Allosaurus*. Would *Barosaurus* really have been able to do this? Perhaps, judging from the strongly constructed leg bones and the base of its tail. But no one knows for sure. It is the job of paleontologists to make accurate guesses, based on the study of the dinosaur's remains.

# HEAVY LIZARD

*Barosaurus* was one of the tallest of the dinosaurs. Standing on all four legs, it could reach treetops as high as a three-story building. Standing up on its back legs, it could reach as high as a five-story building! Its long neck was held up by strong but lightweight bones. And because of its length, scientists think it might have had special valves in its blood vessels to make sure enough blood reached its brain. *Barosaurus* skeletons have been found in North America and Africa but no complete skull has yet been discovered.

*Barosaurus* (barrow-saw-rus) means "heavy lizard."

## Little and large

Dinosaurs came in all shapes and sizes; they were not all giants like *Barosaurus*. Some dinosaurs were as small as the modern-day chicken, while some, such as *Struthiomimus*, were the size of a horse, and others, such as *Heterodontosaurus*, were the size of a dog!

*Barosaurus* had a neck 30 ft (9 m) long, even longer than the necks of *Diplodocus* and *Apatosaurus*, its close relatives. With such a long neck, plant-eating *Barosaurus* could feed far away from where it stood.

*Struthiomimus* "lizard-hipped" dinosaur

## Lizard-hipped

*Barosaurus* was a "lizard-hipped" or saurischian dinosaur. One of the two lower bones of its pelvis pointed forwards, and the other pointed backwards.

*Barosaurus* walked on four legs, which were positioned directly beneath its body.

## Dinosaurs through the ages

*Barosaurus* lived in the Jurassic Period, long before *Tyrannosaurus rex*, which lived at the end of the Cretaceous Period.

**TRIASSIC PERIOD**
248–205 million years ago

**JURASSIC PERIOD**
205–144 million years ago

**CRETACEOUS PERIOD**
144–65 million years ago

## Prehistoric feeder

*Barosaurus* was a plant-eater, or herbivore, belonging to a group of dinosaurs called the sauropods. *Barosaurus* had a huge barrel-shaped body, designed to hold the large amounts of food it ate every day.

## FACT FILE

- **Lived:** 150 million years ago, Jurassic Period
- **Family:** Diplodocids, part of sauropod group
- **Dinosaur type:** Lizard-hipped (saurischian)
- **Maximum life span:** Perhaps 100 years
- **Diet:** Rough plant material
- **Weight when alive:** About 25 tons (25 tonnes)
- **Height:** 50 ft (over 15 m), from ground to head-level
- **Length:** 80 ft (24 m)
- **Top speed:** Over 4 mph (about 7 km/h)

*Barosaurus* had a whiplike tail, which it may have used to frighten off attackers.

## Heavy weight

*Barosaurus* weighed more than eight elephants. It had sturdy, pillar-like legs, which ended in elephant-like feet with five toes. Its back legs were even bigger than its front legs.

# FOSSIL TREASURES

One of the world's richest hoards of dinosaur fossil treasure was discovered among stony, barren hills in Utah. A wide river flowed there in the Jurassic Period, where dinosaurs gathered to eat and drink. Over many years, dinosaur remains were buried under mud and sand and were slowly transformed into fossils.

In 1908, Earl Douglass, a fossil collector, first came to investigate the site for the Carnegie Museum of Natural History. Four years later, he found an almost complete skeleton of *Barosaurus*. Douglass' discoveries were so important that in 1915 the dinosaur graveyard was made a national monument.

### 1 Fit and feeding
*Barosaurus* feeds on ferns and horsetails on the bank of a broad river.

### 2 Death bed
Killed by disease, attack, or drowning, the body of *Barosaurus* has been washed by floodwaters onto a sandbank in the river.

### 3 Buried underground
Thousands of years later, most of the skeleton of *Barosaurus* lies buried under sand, mud, and gravel. Only bones remain. The dinosaur's soft flesh has long since rotted away.

**Journey through time**
*Barosaurus* died in the Late Jurassic Period. Its fossilized skeleton was preserved deep in the Earth for 150 million years until its discovery in 1912.

## DINOSAUR DETECTIVE
### *Earl Douglass (1862 – 1931)*

Earl Douglass was a skilled hunter of dinosaur fossils. In 1908, he discovered the important fossil site later named Dinosaur National Monument. For 16 years he worked to establish the Monument as a unique working museum.

| | |
|---|---|
| 1862 | *Born in Medford, Minnesota.* |
| 1902 | *Joined the staff of the Carnegie Museum, Pittsburgh, Pennsylvania.* |
| 1909 | *Found and began to excavate Apatosaurus.* |
| 1909/24 | *Excavated Apatosaurus, Stegosaurus, Allosaurus, Diplodocus, Camarasaurus, Barosaurus, and Camptosaurus.* |
| 1912/14 | *Excavated skeleton of Barosaurus.* |
| 1914 | *Completed mount of Apatosaurus at the Carnegie Museum.* |
| 1924 | *Left the Dinosaur National Monument.* |
| 1931 | *Died in Salt Lake City, Utah, age 69.* |

**Fossil hunter**
*Earl Douglass, standing next to a partly excavated Diplodocus skeleton in 1922.*

The vertebrae of *Barosaurus*' neck are the most distinctive parts of its skeleton. Each giant fossil vertebra can weigh up to 20 lb (10 kg).

## 6 Heavy work

Centuries of wind and rain have carved the rock of the former riverbed into a landscape of rugged hills and gulleys. Weathering has finally exposed the fragile *Barosaurus* fossils.

## 5 Rising to the surface

The sea has long gone. Movements deep in the Earth's crust over 60 million years have pushed up mountains and tilted the rocks of the ancient riverbed, where the bones of *Barosaurus* now lie closer to the surface.

## 4 Bones to stones

Millions of years later, all the dinosaurs have died. Sea now covers the land where they lived. Chemicals in the layers of rock have slowly turned the dinosaur bones into hard, stony fossils.

**Discovery site of *Barosaurus***

*Fossil photography*
*Recording the scene at camp in the early days of dinosaur discovery.*

Dinosaur National
Monument, Utah

## Buried treasure

The fossil graveyard known as Dinosaur National Monument lies in a great fossil-rich rock unit called the Morrison Formation. This formation stretches all the way from New Mexico to Canada.

# DINOSAUR JIGSAW

Earl Douglass and his team of dinosaur diggers took two long years to excavate the bones of *Barosaurus* on behalf of the Carnegie Museum in Pittsburgh, Pennsylvania. The Museum, however, traded sections of the skeleton with two other museums needing parts to help complete their own sauropod specimens. The fossil bones might still be separated today, were it not for the determination of the dinosaur hunter Barnum Brown. He succeeded in reuniting the complete *Barosaurus* skeleton at the American Museum of Natural History in New York.

Cracks in the ancient fossil bones were repaired with glue and plaster.

### Digging for dinosaurs
Douglass and his men used shovels, hammers, picks, chisels, and even dynamite to dig the fossil skeleton of *Barosaurus* from its rocky grave.

### Controlled explosion
Dynamite was needed to blast away some of the hardest rock. This was formed from the mud and sand of the ancient riverbed, now turned to solid stone.

### Grid system
The fossil bones were excavated from a steep quarry face. A grid was painted on the rock to make it easier to record where each bone was found.

Neck vertebra, slightly crushed during fossilization.

Rounded end of bone fit snugly into the hollow of the next vertebra.

### Plaster jackets
Once exposed, the fragile bones were wrapped in a protective jacket of plaster and burlap. When the plaster was dry, the heavy bones were hauled up the steep rockface.

### Slow sled
Mules dragged the bones in their plaster jackets out of the quarry by sled. Many trips were needed to remove all the fossil bones.

Back vertebra, about 24 in (60 cm) long

### Rock waste
Tons of rock were chipped away from the rockface during the excavation. Waste rubble was pushed in carts along a short railway and then dumped down the steep hillside.

### Fossil trading
Barnum Brown of the American Museum of Natural History in New York had reunited all the parts of the *Barosaurus* skeleton by 1929.

### American Museum of Natural History, New York
This museum used money and fossils to "buy" all parts of the *Barosaurus* skeleton.

### Carnegie Museum, Pittsburgh, Pennsylvania
This museum had received part of *Barosaurus'* tail from the University of Utah.

### Smithsonian Institution, Washington, D.C.
The Smithsonian owned bones from the neck and body of *Barosaurus* and part of a limb.

### University of Utah, Salt Lake City, Utah
The university museum received $5,000 and a fossil horse skeleton in exchange for their *Barosaurus* parts.

### Dinosaur National Monument, Utah
The original site of excavation of *Barosaurus*. Its fossils were later split up among three different museums.

### Basement storage
The *Barosaurus* bones were stored in the basement of the AMNH, where they were available for study. Sixty years later, the Museum finally decided to prepare the fossils for display.

Bones were stored on open shelves in the Museum's basement.

All pieces of fossil from the skeleton were kept together.

These shelves were filled with *Barosaurus* vertebrae.

## DINOSAUR DETECTIVE
### *Barnum Brown (1873 – 1963)*

Barnum Brown was a great dinosaur hunter and collector. In his years at the American Museum of Natural History in New York, he filled the dinosaur halls with many of the fossil skeletons he had excavated. Although he did not discover *Barosaurus* himself, he knew that this was an important specimen to acquire for the Museum's dinosaur collection.

1873  *Born in Carbondale, Kansas.*
1897  *Joined the staff of the American Museum of Natural History (AMNH) in New York.*
1900  *Discovered the world's first known specimen of* **Tyrannosaurus rex.**
1908  *Discovered a second, more complete, specimen of* **Tyrannosaurus rex.**
1910  *Began collecting dinosaur remains along the Red Deer River, Alberta, Canada.*
1912  *Discovered the skeletons of the duck-billed dinosaur,* **Corythosaurus,** *and the horned dinosaur,* **Centrosaurus.**
1916  *Completed dinosaur hunting along the Red Deer River.*
1929  *Gathered the separated parts of the* **Barosaurus** *skeleton at the AMNH.*
1934  *Excavated the remains of over 20 sauropod dinosaurs at Howe Quarry, Wyoming.*
1942  *Retired from the AMNH.*
1963  *Died, age 89, in New York.*

# DINOSAUR DOUBLE

The skeleton of *Barosaurus* was finally taken out of storage 80 years after its discovery. Museum scientists planned to put the bones on display. They wanted to mount the skeleton rearing up on its back legs, defending its young against an attacking *Allosaurus*. Because the fossil bones were fragile and too heavy to display in this way, the scientists decided to make a lightweight plastic replica of the skeleton. Once the fossils had been restored and any missing bones modeled from special clay, casting could begin.

**Materials used to cast the fossilized bones**

Liquid rubber

Liquid plastic

Brushes

Cleaning fluid for brushes

## 1 Building dams
First, "dams" made of cardboard are used to divide the surface of each fossil bone, or group of bones. The dams stand like walls on the surface of the bone, and split it into sections. More dams are needed if the bone shape is complicated. The dams give flat edges to the molds, so that all the parts of a replica bone will fit together neatly.

## 2 Making a rubber mold
Each part of the fossil bone and dam is now painted with layers of liquid rubber. When the rubber sets, it forms a perfect, flexible mold of the original bone's surface. The rubber mold is then peeled away from the fossil.

## 3 Supporting the mold
The rubber mold is strengthened with cotton gauze. A plastic jacket is made to support the outside.

## 4 Casting the bones
Next, the inside of the rubber mold is coated with liquid plastic. The plastic will duplicate every detail that has been molded from the fossil's surface.

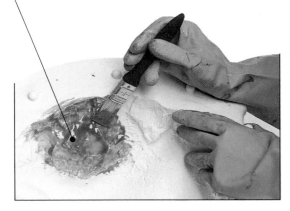

## 5 Assembling the cast
Sheets of fiberglass are added to the plastic to make light but strong casts of the fossil. The cast sections are then joined together to recreate the entire bone's shape.

## 6 Filling the cast
The hollow bone cast is made even stronger by pouring in a special liquid foam plastic. This foam hardens to form a tough honeycomb center.

## 7 Removing the mold
When the foam plastic has hardened inside the cast, the rubber mold and its supporting jacket are peeled away from the outside. At last, a perfectly shaped plastic copy of the original fossil bone is revealed.

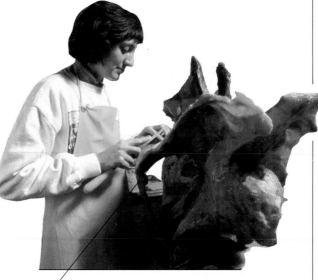

## 8 Finishing touches
Finally, the rough edges left by the joints between the separate mold sections are carefully filed away. The plastic bone is then painted to match the colors of the original fossil.

## 9 Measuring up
The replica fossils are measured against a chart of the whole skeleton. Each plastic bone is then matched up against its neighbors to check the fit. Only when all the bones are complete – more than 200 – will the lightweight *Barosaurus* skeleton be ready for assembly in the museum.

# BUILDING BAROSAURUS

The *Barosaurus* skeleton was hauled by truck from Canada to New York for assembly in its new home at the American Museum of Natural History. Here, the task of assembling the *Barosaurus* mount in its unique rearing pose required expert construction skills. Specialists from many different fields – artists and model-makers, paleontologists, and engineers – all came together to reconstruct a dramatic scene that may have taken place around 150 million years ago.

A few of the many dinosaur builders whose varied skills helped to assemble the rearing *Barosaurus* mount.

**1 The skeleton arrives**
Huge trucks deliver the replica *Barosaurus* bones safely to the museum.

**2 Checking the plans**
Inside the museum, detailed plans are consulted at each stage of the dinosaur's assembly. Even a small mistake in the positioning of body sections would be difficult to correct, once building is complete.

**3 Dinosaur rib cage**
The giant rib cage is unloaded in one piece. The ribs show the barrel shape of *Barosaurus'* vast body.

**4 Neck section**
The massive neck section is gently removed from the trailer. The giant vertebrae are already threaded onto a supporting steel pipe.

**5 Rocky base**
A natural landscape is pieced together to make a realistic base for the *Barosaurus* mount. Latex rubber was painted onto rocky ground in Montana. When set, the rubber was peeled away and used as a mold to make a fiberglass cast, or "land-peel."

**6 "Land-peel" scene**
The "land-peel" is assembled before building begins. It will help recreate the scene of 150 million years ago.

**7 Lifting platform**
The rear legs and upper pelvis of *Barosaurus* are raised into the air using a lifting platform. The platform allows the dinosaur builders to gently lower the heavy legs onto the framework below.

**8 Tail piece**
Before the legs are finally put in place, the tail sections are moved into position. The supporting metal frame is then welded together.

**10 Filling in the gaps**
Shielded from the hot, flying sparks by his helmet, a welder works quickly to join the steel frame running through *Barosaurus'* tail sections. A vertebra is then placed over each welded joint.

**9 Welding the framework**
The skeleton of the young *Barosaurus* is assembled in the foreground, as the steel rods of the mother's tail are welded together.

# HIGH-RISE SKELETON

The most dramatic stage in the reconstruction of *Barosaurus* was the joining of the long neck section to the rest of the skeleton. The rearing replica was designed to stand over 50 ft (15 m) tall, and so this stage called for dinosaur builders who did not fear heights!

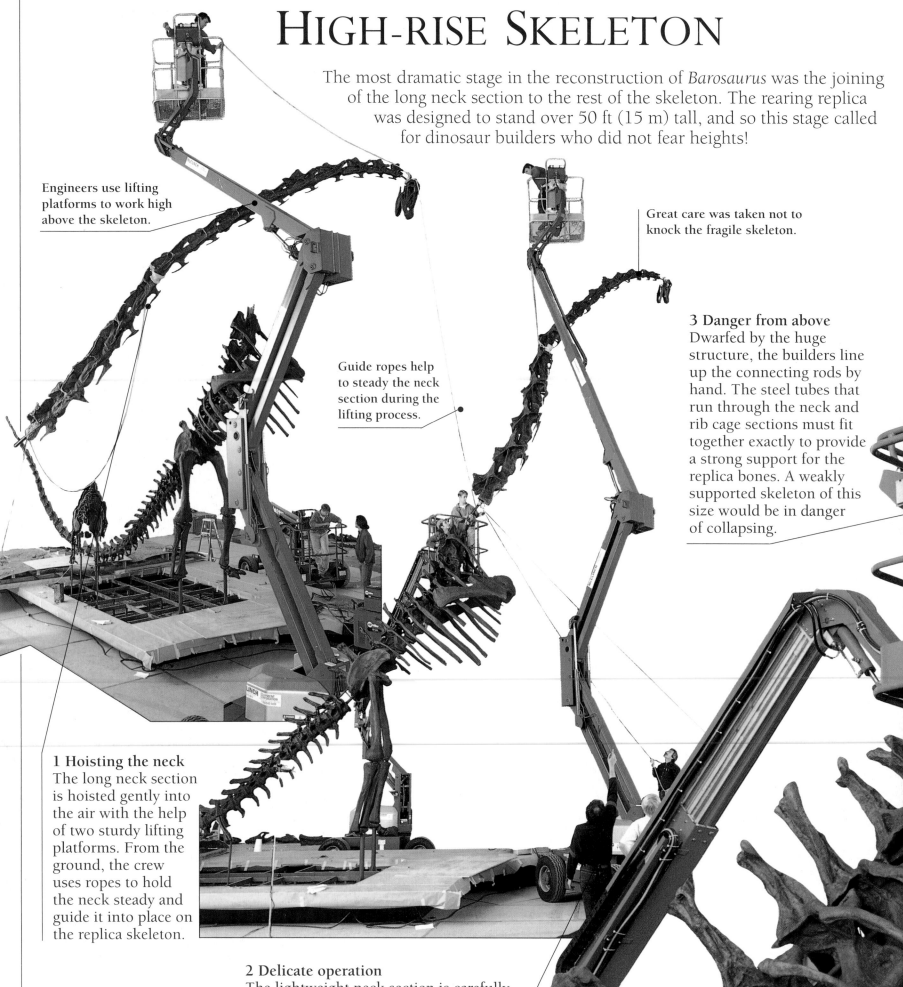

Engineers use lifting platforms to work high above the skeleton.

Great care was taken not to knock the fragile skeleton.

Guide ropes help to steady the neck section during the lifting process.

**3 Danger from above**
Dwarfed by the huge structure, the builders line up the connecting rods by hand. The steel tubes that run through the neck and rib cage sections must fit together exactly to provide a strong support for the replica bones. A weakly supported skeleton of this size would be in danger of collapsing.

**1 Hoisting the neck**
The long neck section is hoisted gently into the air with the help of two sturdy lifting platforms. From the ground, the crew uses ropes to hold the neck steady and guide it into place on the replica skeleton.

**2 Delicate operation**
The lightweight neck section is carefully lowered into position over the upright rib cage. The crew below watches anxiously.

Every section,
including the giant
neck vertebrae, is
lightweight and
filled with foam.

**4 Safely in place**
At last, workers on the lower-level
lifting platform signal that
the neck and head section is
slotted firmly into place.

During welding, the
replica fossil bones
are protected with
fireproof cloth.

**5 Finishing touches**
The steel supports of the neck are
welded together. Care is taken to
shield the bones from hot sparks,
which could set them on fire.
Another stage in this daring
reconstruction is complete.

# ATTACK AND DEFENSE

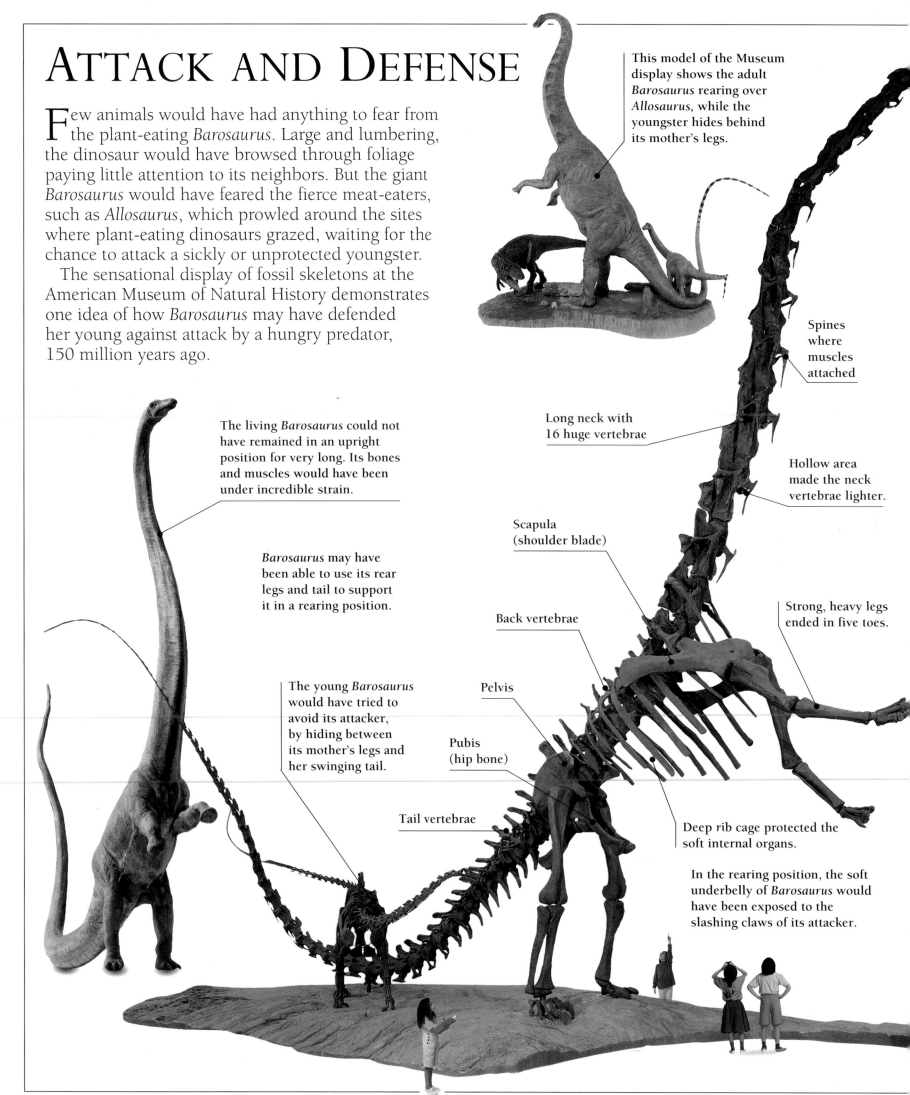

Few animals would have had anything to fear from the plant-eating *Barosaurus*. Large and lumbering, the dinosaur would have browsed through foliage paying little attention to its neighbors. But the giant *Barosaurus* would have feared the fierce meat-eaters, such as *Allosaurus*, which prowled around the sites where plant-eating dinosaurs grazed, waiting for the chance to attack a sickly or unprotected youngster.

The sensational display of fossil skeletons at the American Museum of Natural History demonstrates one idea of how *Barosaurus* may have defended her young against attack by a hungry predator, 150 million years ago.

This model of the Museum display shows the adult *Barosaurus* rearing over *Allosaurus*, while the youngster hides behind its mother's legs.

Spines where muscles attached

Long neck with 16 huge vertebrae

Hollow area made the neck vertebrae lighter.

The living *Barosaurus* could not have remained in an upright position for very long. Its bones and muscles would have been under incredible strain.

Scapula (shoulder blade)

*Barosaurus* may have been able to use its rear legs and tail to support it in a rearing position.

Back vertebrae

Strong, heavy legs ended in five toes.

The young *Barosaurus* would have tried to avoid its attacker, by hiding between its mother's legs and her swinging tail.

Pelvis

Pubis (hip bone)

Deep rib cage protected the soft internal organs.

Tail vertebrae

In the rearing position, the soft underbelly of *Barosaurus* would have been exposed to the slashing claws of its attacker.

The head of *Barosaurus* was modeled on that of *Diplodocus*, its close relative. A few *Barosaurus* skull bones have been found, but only in Africa. A complete skull has never been discovered.

**Fast runner**
The replica skeleton of *Allosaurus* is mounted in a running position, with its tail outstretched for balance.

**1 Base framework**
The body and tail are attached to the legs and pelvis, which are mounted on a metal framework.

*Allosaurus* had small, powerful front limbs. Each hand had three sharp claws.

*Allosaurus* stood upright like a bird, on three long toes.

**2 Arms in place**
The bones of the shoulders, arms, and the dangerous claws are welded into place.

**Hungry hunter**
150 million years ago, *Allosaurus* was the chief predator in the land that is now North America. *Allosaurus* was 36 ft (11 m) long and weighed 1.5 tons (1.5 tonnes). It posed a deadly threat to a young *Barosaurus*.

Tail held high for balance

Large, powerful legs for running after prey

**3 Skull and bones**
The skull of *Allosaurus*, four times longer than a human head, is placed at the end of the smoothly curved neck. The replica skeleton is now complete.

Jaws lined with razor-sharp teeth for cutting and tearing flesh

The natural landscape base helps to set the scene of the Jurassic Period.

# ON THE MOVE

Barosaurus lived at a time when the climate was warm with wet and dry seasons. Thick layers of mudstones, river sands, and gravels found in the ancient rocks at the Dinosaur National Monument show there were periods of heavy rain and floods. Fossilized mud cracks indicate there were also times of drought. *Barosaurus*, as all animals, needed a regular food supply. For this reason, during droughts, the plant-eating dinosaurs of the Jurassic Period might have left behind the dead and drying plants in search of fresh feeding grounds, just as animals migrate over the African plains today.

**High-rise defense**
Some scientists believe that sauropod dinosaurs like *Barosaurus* could rear up on their hind legs in defense against an attacker. Their tails may have been used as leverage and for support.

**Steps in time**
Scientists have unearthed fossilized dinosaur footprints, left in soft sand and mud, which suggest how quickly the animals moved. Prints made by *Barosaurus* itself have not been identified, but other sauropod footprints suggest they may have walked at speeds of over 4 mph (about 7 km/h).

Sets of fossil dinosaur footprints suggest that many sauropods traveled in herds.

Although very few skeletons of *Barosaurus* have been found, it is probable that like its relatives, it traveled in herds.

The absence of trails left by tails among dinosaur footprints indicates that sauropods walked with their tails held up off the ground.

Patterns of dinosaur footprints recently found suggest that young dinosaurs walked behind the adults when traveling in a herd.

### Long-distance link
Sauropod remains have been found in Tanzania in Africa, as well as in South Dakota and Wyoming in North America. This fossil evidence shows that the continents of Africa and North America must have formed one land mass during the middle Jurassic Period.

43

# GREEDY GIANT

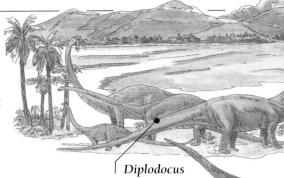

*Barosaurus* was a giant plant-eater living during the Jurassic Period. The warm, wet climate produced the great quantity of plants needed to satisfy this dinosaur's monster appetite. Although there were no grasses, *Barosaurus* and other herbivores fed on ferns, horsetails, ginkgos, conifers, and many other plants that still grow today.

*Diplodocus*

### Gentle grazers
Many dinosaurs grazed with *Barosaurus* on the lush floodplain or along the winding river.

*Barosaurus* needed to eat huge amounts of plant food every day to fuel its gigantic body.

### Stony stomach
*Barosaurus* raked in plant matter with its peglike teeth and then swallowed it whole. Once in its stomach, the food was ground into a thick paste by hard, shiny pebbles called gastroliths.

*Barosaurus* swallowed stones to grind up its food, just as some birds do today.

### Treetop browser
The long neck of *Barosaurus* was useful for feeding on leaves high in the treetops. Instead of browsing at such a dizzying height, it might have preferred leaves from lower branches.

### Whiplash tail
*Barosaurus* stayed on constant alert when near a prowling *Allosaurus*. If the *Allosaurus* threatened to attack its young, *Barosaurus* could whip its tail to keep the predator at bay.

*Apatosaurus*

*Camptosaurus*

*Stegosaurus*

**Fast movers**
Small *Dryosaurus* lived
in groups. They relied
on speed to escape
from danger.

**Riverside feeders**
Groups of *Apatosaurus*
and a *Camptosaurus*
browsed by the riverside.

**Hungry herbivores**
Both *Stegosaurus* with its bony
plates, and large herds of the
long-necked *Diplodocus*, grazed
together on the plains.

**Ferocious hunter**
*Allosaurus* was a fierce carnivore
that hunted plant-eaters.

The long neck of *Barosaurus*
allowed its head to move in
all directions, as the animal
watched for danger.

If a baby *Barosaurus*
survived disease and
attack, and found enough
to eat, it might have lived
to be 100 years old.

**Baby food**
The young *Barosaurus* stayed
close to its parent, feeding on
low-growing leaves and ground
plants, such as ferns.

# BAROSAURUS SPECIMEN AND FAMILY FACTS

- **Specimen number:** AMNH 6341
- **Excavated by:** Earl Douglass
- **Excavation:** 1912–1914, at Dinosaur National Monument, Utah
- **Bones found:** Four-fifths of skeleton, but no complete skull. Skull modeled on *Diplodocus*, its close relative

- **Where displayed:** American Museum of Natural History, New York City
- **Year when constructed:** 1991; lightweight replica bones modeled in plastic and metal, used in place of original and valuable heavy fossils

---

## 🏛 ON THE MUSEUM TRAIL 🏛

### A museum guide to sauropod specimens
A partial listing of collections, including both fossils and replica casts of fossils.

**UNITED STATES**
(*Diplodocus*) Pratt Museum (Amherst College), Amherst, Massachusetts
(*Apatosaurus*) Field Museum of Natural History, Chicago, Illinois
(*Diplodocus*) Houston Museum of Natural Sciences, Houston, Texas
(*Apatosaurus, Diplodocus*) Dinosaur National Monument, Jensen, Utah
(*Apatosaurus*) The Geological Museum, Laramie, Wyoming
(*Apatosaurus, Barosaurus*) American Museum of Natural History, New York, New York
(*Apatosaurus*) Peabody Museum of Natural History, Yale University, Connecticut
(*Supersaurus*) Academy of Natural Sciences, Philadelphia, Pennsylvania
(*Apatosaurus, Diplodocus*) Carnegie Museum of Natural History, Pittsburgh, Pennsylvania

Sauropod specimens may also be found in museums in Argentina, Canada, China, France, Germany, Italy, Japan, Mexico, Mongolia, Morocco, Russia, Spain, and the United Kingdom.

**Unique display**
The AMNH in New York has the only *Barosaurus* skeleton on display in the world. A replica made of plastic and metal, the dinosaur rears up in the air, protecting its young from an attacking *Allosaurus*.

(*Supersaurus*) Earth Science Museum, Brigham Young University, Provo, Utah
(*Diplodocus*) The Science Museum of Minnesota, St Paul, Minnesota
(*Barosaurus*) Utah Museum of Natural History, University of Utah, Salt Lake City, Utah
(*Diplodocus*) Utah Natural History State Museum, Vernal, Utah
(*Diplodocus*) National Museum of Natural History, Smithsonian Institution, Washington, D.C.

*Barosaurus* had a neck 30 ft long ( 9 m). This animal lived around 150 million years ago, during the Jurassic Period.

## Dinosaur world

The sauropod dinosaurs were the largest animals ever to live on land. Their fossils have been discovered on all the continents except Antarctica. This map shows where some members of the sauropod family have been found.

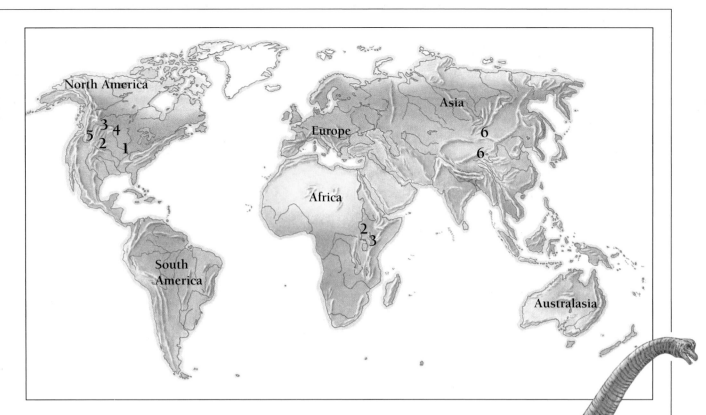

### Key to map

1   *Apatosaurus*
2   *Barosaurus*
3   *Brachiosaurus*
4   *Camarasaurus*
5   *Diplodocus*
6   *Mamenchisaurus*

## Family trees

*Barosaurus* belongs to the diplodocid family, like *Apatosaurus* and *Diplodocus*. *Mamenchisaurus* was a close relative but *Brachiosaurus* and *Camarasaurus* were only distant cousins. All of them belong to a larger group of dinosaurs called the sauropods. Most sauropods lived during the Late Jurassic Period.

*Mamenchisaurus* had the longest neck known of all the dinosaurs. It lived at about the same time as *Barosaurus*, during the Late Jurassic Period.

*Brachiosaurus* was taller than most dinosaurs. It also lived in the Late Jurassic Period.

*Apatosaurus* was shorter than *Barosaurus* and lived at the same time and in the same area.

*Diplodocus* was one of the longest dinosaurs. It also lived with *Barosaurus* in what is now North America.

*Camarasaurus* was a bulky sauropod that lived alongside *Barosaurus*.

The remains of *Barosaurus* have been found in North America and in Africa. A few skull bones have been discovered in Africa, but no complete *Barosaurus* skull has yet been found.

# CORYTHOSAURUS

*Corythosaurus* lived around 75 million years ago in western North America. It belonged to a large group of plant-eating dinosaurs called hadrosaurs, or duck-billed dinosaurs. Hadrosaurs were social animals that lived in herds. They can be divided into two groups: dinosaurs with spectacular head crests like *Corythosaurus*, and flat-headed dinosaurs without crests.

By studying the helmet-shaped crest on the skull of *Corythosaurus*, scientists can gather clues about the dinosaur's lifestyle. Exciting research in the last few years has looked at hadrosaur fossils in light of what we know about today's animals that live in herds. Members of a hadrosaur herd could recognize each other by their head crest shape, and they could probably distinguish between sexes in this way, too. The crests were hollow and enabled *Corythosaurus* to make loud trumpeting noises so that large herds could keep in touch with each other by sound as well as sight.

However, there is much that we still do not know about *Corythosaurus*. For instance, how many years did a newly hatched baby take to grow up? How long did one of these dinosaurs live? These are questions that we cannot yet answer. However, scientific methods of the future as well as new fossil finds may provide the answers and reveal more about these fascinating animals from the past.

# HELMET LIZARD

*Corythosaurus* was a crested member of the duck-billed family of plant-eating dinosaurs. It lived around 75 to 72 million years ago, near the end of the dinosaurs' reign. The crest on top of a *Corythosaurus'* head grew from hatching and varied in size. Enough fossils have been discovered for scientists to distinguish differences between the crests of male and female adults, and also between adults and babies. It is thought that an adult male's was larger than the female's and roughly the size and shape of half a dinner plate.

**Duck-billed dinosaurs**
*Corythosaurus* was a member of the hadrosaur family of dinosaurs. Hadrosaurs are nicknamed "duck-bills" because of their broad, duck-like beaks. Some hadrosaurs grew up to 49 ft long (15 m), although *Corythosaurus* itself reached only 24 ft (7.5 m).

**Dinosaur skin color**
No one knows what color the markings on dinosaur skin may have been. Some dinosaurs may have been colored for camouflage, while others may have been brightly patterned to warn off predators. The markings shown here are one interpretation of how *Corythosaurus* may have looked.

*Corythosaurus* (korrith-oh-saw-rus) means "helmet lizard" after the hollow bony helmet-like crest on the dinosaur's head.

A curved, flexible neck helped *Corythosaurus* to turn its head to feed among tree branches.

*Corythosaurus* could run upright on two legs or drop down on all fours.

The tail of the *Corythosaurus* was not very flexible. It could probably move only a little from side to side. The tail was held up off the ground behind the body and helped *Corythosaurus* to keep its balance when walking on two legs.

## FACT FILE

- **Lived:** Between 75-72 million years ago, during the Cretaceous Period
- **Family:** Hadrosaurids, the duck-billed dinosaurs
- **Dinosaur type:** Bird-hipped (ornithischian)
- **Diet:** Plant material, such as leaves, fruit, and seeds
- **Weight when alive:** Over 4 tons (about 4 tonnes)
- **Height:** Approximately 10 ft (3 m)
- **Length:** Approximately 24 ft (7.5 m)
- **Top speed:** possibly 20 mph (up to 32 km/h)

The toothless beak and hundreds of grinding teeth are signs that *Corythosaurus* was a plant-eater, or herbivore. Fossilized plant remains, such as pine needles and cones, have been found with hadrosaur skeletons.

Hoof-shaped claws and padded toes show that the dinosaur's front limbs were used mainly for walking.

### Bird-hipped
*Corythosaurus* was a "bird-hipped" or ornithischian dinosaur. Both of its lower hip bones pointed down and backwards.

*Iguanodon* "bird-hipped" dinosaur

### Dinosaur times
*Corythosaurus* lived towards the end of the Earth's Cretaceous Period, before *Tyrannosaurus rex* but long after *Barosaurus,* which lived in the Jurassic Period.

**TRIASSIC PERIOD**
248–205 million years ago

**JURASSIC PERIOD**
205–144 million years ago

**CRETACEOUS PERIOD**
144–65 million years ago

51

# DINOSAUR DISCOVERY

In 1914, the famous dinosaur hunter, Barnum Brown, made a sensational find. He noticed fossil bones weathering out of rocks along the Red Deer River, near Steveville, Alberta, Canada. The bones were part of a beautifully preserved *Corythosaurus* skeleton – only the end of the tail and parts of the hands were missing.

Two years earlier, Brown had unearthed the first known specimen of *Corythosaurus*, but this second find was more complete. The bones were partly crushed, but they were still lying in their original positions, as if *Corythosaurus* had carefully lain down to die in soft, sandy mud, about 75 million years before.

## Bones to stones
When animals and plants are buried underground, they are sometimes changed into hard replicas of themselves, called fossils. This change may take place over millions of years as chemicals in rocks and soil seep into the buried object.

## 1 Food and drink
About 75 million years ago, *Corythosaurus* pauses by a winding stream on a wide, flat plain. It feasts on the conifers, ferns, and flowers that grow there.

## 2 Muddy waters
A few years later, *Corythosaurus* lies dead on the bank of a river. The rains falling in the distant mountains will soon flood the river, sweeping mud and sand over the animal carcass.

## 3 Buried dinosaur
Over hundreds of years, the rivers move back and forward across the plain, building up layers of mud and sand over the buried skeleton. Other dinosaurs now live above ground.

Tibia (shin bone)

**Corythosaurus fossil**
Only the hard parts of the *Corythosaurus* skeleton, such as the bones and teeth, were fossilized. The softer flesh and skin were not preserved, but rotted away in the damp soil soon after the dinosaur's death.

Over millions of years, *Corythosaurus*' bones are buried deeper and deeper underground.

# DINOSAUR DETECTIVE

## Barnum Brown (1873 – 1963)

Barnum Brown was one of the world's greatest dinosaur hunters. He found his first dinosaur fossil, a *Triceratops* skull, in 1895 and went on to fill the American Museum of Natural History (AMNH) in New York with many finds.

| | |
|---|---|
| 1873 | *Born in Carbondale, Kansas.* |
| 1897 | *Joined AMNH as a paleontologist, age 24.* |
| 1900 | *Discovered the first known remains of* **Tyrannosaurus rex**. |
| 1910 | *Leads expedition to hunt dinosaurs by boat along the Red Deer River, Alberta, Canada.* |
| 1912 | *Discovered the first* **Corythosaurus** *near Steveville, Alberta.* |
| 1914 | *Discovered a more complete specimen of* **Corythosaurus**. |
| 1963 | *Died in New York, at the age of 89.* |

*Barnum Brown (to the right) on his flatboat on the Red Deer River*

## Dinosaur Provincial Park

Over 350 fossil skeletons, including that of *Corythosaurus*, have been found near the Red Deer River in Alberta, Canada. So many have been discovered that the area has been set aside as a dinosaur park.

Discovery site of *Corythosaurus*

Red Deer River, near Steveville, Alberta, Canada

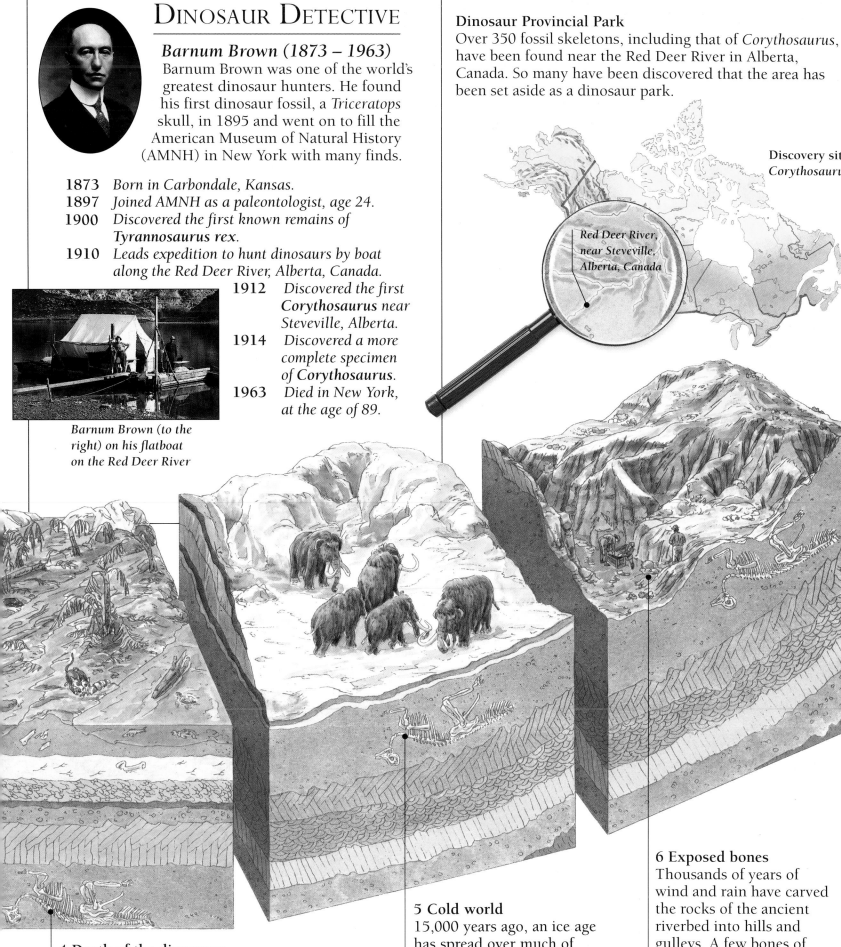

## 4 Death of the dinosaurs

65 million years ago, the dinosaurs have become extinct. The skeleton slowly turns to fossil as chemicals pass from the rocks into the bones.

## 5 Cold world

15,000 years ago, an ice age has spread over much of North America. Huge earth movements have pushed the rocks and the fossilized bones closer to the surface.

## 6 Exposed bones

Thousands of years of wind and rain have carved the rocks of the ancient riverbed into hills and gulleys. A few bones of the fossilized *Corythosaurus* have weathered out of the steep side of a canyon.

# FRAGILE FIND

In 1909, Barnum Brown visited a ranch near the Red Deer River in Alberta, Canada. The ranch owner had found fossils high up in the barren canyons near his home. Brown identified the fossils as dinosaur bones and mounted an expedition on behalf of his employer, the American Museum of Natural History in New York.

Between 1910 and 1915, Barnum Brown and his team of dinosaur hunters used a flatboat, or barge, to travel down the river, going ashore to look for fossils in the nearby cliffs. In the summer of 1914, Brown and his colleagues excavated their best find, the well-preserved skeleton of an adult *Corythosaurus*.

**1 Hunter's camp**
Far from any town, the fossil hunters had to sleep in tents on the riverbank. Life was harsh, and the men often wore nets over their heads to protect them from mosquito bites. All meals were cooked in a tent on the flatboat. Each day, the team sailed farther down the river, stopping to go ashore and explore the steep canyons along the riverbanks.

**2 Hard labor**
In 1914, Brown noticed some fossil bones on an exposed rockface. Brown and his team began to dig the rock from around the bones. Before long, he had uncovered the nearly complete skeleton of a *Corythosaurus*.

When the rock was cleared away, the tailbones were found still connected.

**3 Fossil discovery**
After months of backbreaking work, the fragile fossils of *Corythosaurus* were finally uncovered. The fossils were riddled with cracks and gaps, but the shapes of the animal's limbs and tail were visible. Still partly attached to lumps of rock, the crumbling bones were carefully painted with glue to preserve their shape.

## 5 Heavy fossils
The huge blocks of rock and plaster containing the *Corythosaurus* skeleton were too heavy to lift by hand. Wooden beams, ropes, and pulleys were used to lift the massive blocks, lower them into strong, straw-lined crates, and then load them onto horse-drawn wagons.

## 4 Broken bones
Each block of rock containing the fragile fossils was wrapped in a protective jacket of plaster and burlap for the long journey to the museum in New York. The jackets would be removed when scientists began to prepare the bones for museum display.

## 6 Wagon train
The difficult journey by horse and cart to the railroad station often took many days. Many tons of fossils were carried in this way over the rough, barren landscape.

The bones of the dinosaur's spine and neck, still covered with stone.

Part of the dinosaur's skeleton still lies buried.

The arm bones have been well preserved, but parts of the hand were lost before the animal's carcass was buried.

Rear leg of *Corythosaurus*

The bones of the right leg and foot partly conceal those on the other side.

## 7 Skeleton restoration
Back at the museum in New York, scientists first removed the plaster jackets from the broken bones, then glued them together and filled the gaps with plaster. Years of work were needed to transform the fossil fragments into an almost-perfect dinosaur skeleton.

# SKELETON STORY

The nearly complete skeleton of *Corythosaurus* that Barnum Brown had excavated was finally placed on display at the American Museum of Natural History in New York after many years of painstaking restoration. Each fossil bone had to be chipped free of the surrounding rock, repaired with plaster, and strengthened with glue. The huge, 23-ft long (7.5 m) skeleton was then put together and mounted in its original burial position in a large glass display case.

The skeleton can be identified as *Corythosaurus* by its skull, with a high, flat-sided crest; many rows of teeth; and horny beak. The powerful rear legs would have helped even a large adult *Corythosaurus* to run quite swiftly over short distances, to escape a prowling predator.

Short, slender arms ended in hands shaped like hooves for walking.

**Death of a dinosaur**
Lying on its side, the mounted skeleton captures the moment, millions of years ago, when sand and mud covered the dead body of *Corythosaurus*. The legs, arms, and body shape have been preserved almost undisturbed in the dinosaur's original death pose.

There were over 60 vertebrae in the tail.

Missing parts of the tail may have been washed away by floodwaters before the carcass was buried.

**Bony corset**
Like bird-hipped dinosaurs, *Corythosaurus* had extra scaffolding supporting its body. Long, bony rods, formed from muscle and tendons, crisscrossed along its backbone, over the hips, and into the tail. This bony corset helped *Corythosaurus* to walk upright on two legs but also held its tail stiff, so that it did not swing from side to side.

The long shaft of the ischium (rear hip bone) pointed backward far under the tail.

The large, three-toed feet ended in flattened hooves.

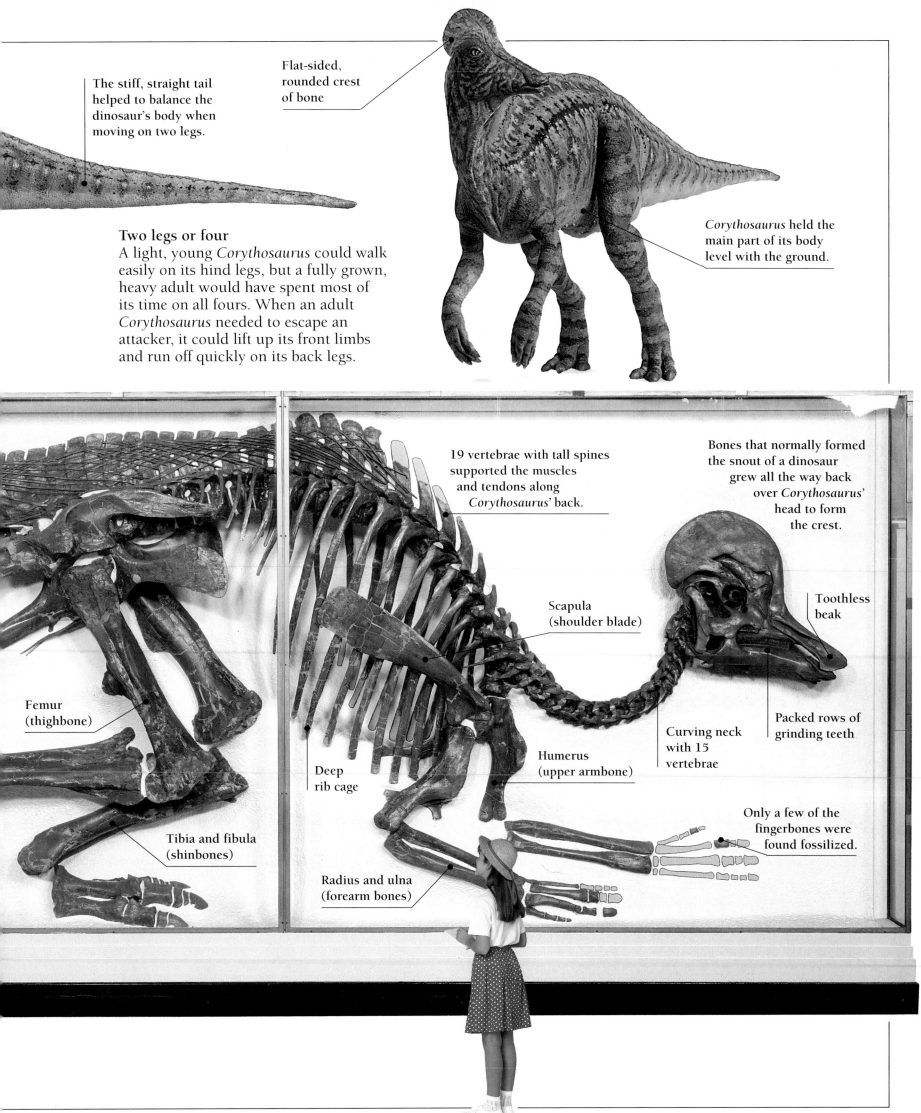

The stiff, straight tail helped to balance the dinosaur's body when moving on two legs.

Flat-sided, rounded crest of bone

*Corythosaurus* held the main part of its body level with the ground.

## Two legs or four

A light, young *Corythosaurus* could walk easily on its hind legs, but a fully grown, heavy adult would have spent most of its time on all fours. When an adult *Corythosaurus* needed to escape an attacker, it could lift up its front limbs and run off quickly on its back legs.

19 vertebrae with tall spines supported the muscles and tendons along *Corythosaurus*' back.

Bones that normally formed the snout of a dinosaur grew all the way back over *Corythosaurus*' head to form the crest.

Scapula (shoulder blade)

Toothless beak

Femur (thighbone)

Packed rows of grinding teeth

Deep rib cage

Curving neck with 15 vertebrae

Humerus (upper armbone)

Tibia and fibula (shinbones)

Only a few of the fingerbones were found fossilized.

Radius and ulna (forearm bones)

# GREEDY GRAZER

During the Late Cretaceous Period, hadrosaurs like the 4-ton (4-tonne) *Corythosaurus* were among the most common dinosaurs of their day. Walking and running on powerful limbs, the duckbills may have traveled in large, fast-moving herds far across the coastal plains of what is now North America. These hungry plant-eaters munched their way through forest after forest of pine trees, ferns, flowers, and broad-leaved trees. Their rows of tightly packed teeth could mash even the toughest twigs into soft pulp, which was easy to swallow and digest.

**1 Reaching for food**
*Corythosaurus'* hooved fingers are shaped for walking, although it can use its hands and arms to pull branches toward its mouth.

The favorite food of *Corythosaurus* may have been trees like conifers and sycamores.

**3 Grinding up food**
*Corythosaurus* leans forward with its beak to snip off a twig. Its jaws squeeze the food between its rows of teeth and grind it up.

The fossilized remains of seeds, pine needles, and twigs have all been found in the stomach of one mummified hadrosaur.

**2 Feasting in the forest**
Ducking its head, *Corythosaurus* sweeps through the bushes, feeding mostly on plants up to 6.5 ft (2 m) tall. It rears up on its hind legs to strip twigs, fruit, and leaves from the taller trees.

*Corythosaurus*' stiff tail did not swing from side to side, perhaps helping it to run fast.

A heavy adult *Corythosaurus* would most often stand and walk on all fours. But at the first sign of danger, it might rise on its back legs, with tail and body held straight, and perhaps run off at the speed of 20 mph (32 km/h).

## Winter fodder

Remains of duck-billed dinosaurs have been found as far north as present-day Alaska. Few plants would have grown here in winter, so duck-billed dinosaurs may have migrated south to warmer areas, in search of fresh food to satisfy their appetite.

## 4 Moving off

*Corythosaurus* stands upright to strip the last branches that it can reach. The trees are left with torn bark and bare branches. It is time for the dinosaur to move on to new feeding grounds.

No fossil evidence shows the original skin color of *Corythosaurus*, but it may have had striking markings, like some birds and reptiles today.

Scientists once thought that *Corythosaurus* had webbed hands. Fossil evidence has revealed that each finger was padded with a tough, fleshy cushion.

# SIGHT AND SMELL

The duckbills, or hadrosaurs, are among the most easily identified of all the dinosaurs. Many of the species, including *Corythosaurus*, were distinguished by spectacular head crests and distinctive mouths. *Corythosaurus'* sharp, rough-edged beak, which may have grown throughout the animal's life, was probably made of horn over bone, like human fingernails. The dinosaur's interlocking rows of teeth were also constantly replaced with new teeth, growing up from the jaw as the old ones wore down. As a group, the hadrosaur family probably had highly developed senses of sight, smell, and hearing to help them pick up messages from other dinosaurs, such as a warning of danger from an approaching predator.

**Dinosaur senses**
Although the brain of *Corythosaurus* seems small for such a large animal, it was well developed. It controlled the senses of sight, smell, and hearing as well as other body functions.

Chamber with smell-detecting part of the brain

Air passage to crest

Brain connected to smell organs

Nostrils let air into the hollow crest.

**Flat-sided skulls**
The skull of *Hypacrosaurus* is easily mistaken for its relative *Corythosaurus*, but it has a less-rounded crest. The skulls of both animals were long and flat-sided, like that of a horse.

Thin, hollow crest was made up of bones growing up from the nose to the back of the skull.

Long, deep hollows on both sides of the skull led to the nostrils.

The wide, bony snout of the living dinosaur was covered with horn, like a duck's beak.

Hundreds of teeth were packed together to make long rasping surfaces, like files, in each jaw.

As the lower jaws shut, they pushed each side of the upper jaws outward. This made the teeth rub together from side to side to grind up food.

## Dinosaur vision

Many predators have eyes that face forward, giving them good vision for hunting or for using their hands.

Like many plant-eating animals, *Corythosaurus* had large eyes on the sides of its head. It could see in two different directions at once and watch for danger over a wide area as it fed.

Scientists do not know, however, if *Corythosaurus* saw in color, as people do, or in shades of gray.

*Corythosaurus* would have seen two separate views of its surroundings at the same time. Its brain made sense of the different view from each side of its head.

The left eye sees a *Euoplocephalus* feeding in the vegetation.

The right eye sees danger from a hungry, prowling *Albertosaurus*.

Left eye

Right eye

## Head signals

Hadrosaurs may have been able to recognize family members from the color markings on their heads and from the differently shaped skulls. They communicated by using the air chambers in their crests to make distinctive hoots and calls.

The bony crest was covered in skin and may have been highly patterned to help hadrosaurs recognize others from the same group.

All *Corythosaurus* crests were flat-sided, but some were smaller than others. Males may have had larger crests than females.

A large eardrum at the back of the head may have helped *Corythosaurus* to hear calls made by other dinosaurs in the area.

# HORNBLOWERS

Few living animals can compete with the amazing head crests sported by the hadrosaur family. Scientists once thought that hadrosaur crests were used as underwater snorkels and airtanks, or that they helped the dinosaurs to smell an approaching attacker. Hadrosaurs could tell males from females, and young dinosaurs from old, by the distinctive size and shape of their crests.

In recent experiments, scientists have tried blowing air through tubes similar to those in hollow hadrosaur crests. Results show that some duckbills could use their crests to call to one another.

The flat headplate was used to make hooting sounds.

Spike at back of skull

Toothless beak

**Lambeosaurus skull**
*Lambeosaurus* may have used the flat-sided, hollow crest on top of its head to make sounds to communicate with other hadrosaurs. There was also a bony prong at the back of its skull.

**Kritosaurus**
Few remains have been found of the duck-billed *Kritosaurus*. It had no crest, except for a small, bony lump in front of its eyes.

Small, bony lump

**Lambeosaurus**
*Lambeosaurus* lived in North America at the same time as *Corythosaurus*. It had a distinctive hollow headplate.

Inflatable skin balloon

**Edmontosaurus**
*Edmontosaurus* had no crest, but it may have had an inflatable skin balloon over its long snout, used to make sounds. Many skulls have been found in the U.S. and Canada.

## Parasaurolophus skull

The skull of *Parasaurolophus* ended in a long, hollow crest. *Parasaurolophus* could use its crest to make loud noises. Animals could be told apart by their distinctive honks or hoots. Females and the young had smaller crests.

The crest contained hollow tubes and was over 3 ft long (1 m).

Some scientists think that a flap of skin may have hung down from the end of the crest.

Air tubes grew from the nostrils over the top of the skull.

Rows of teeth for grinding up food

## Musical creatures

Many animals have crests or flaps of skin to frighten or attract other animals. Some birds have brightly colored feather crests to signal to others of their kind. A few lizards and frogs can inflate a pouch of skin on their throat to attract a mate or to make croaking noises.

The inflatable balloon of some hadrosaurs may have acted like the throat pouch of a bullfrog. Sounds made in a bullfrog's throat are made louder in its pouch and so can be heard far away.

Inflated throat pouch

## Parasaurolophus

*Parasaurolophus* had one of the longest hadrosaur crests. It contained two long, bony tubes that led up from the nostrils.

Bony spike

## Saurolophus

*Saurolophus* may have had inflatable nostrils growing up from its snout. Remains have been found in North America and Mongolia.

The hollow crests and air pouches of hadrosaurs varied in size and length. When calling in a group, these dinosaurs may have produced a range of honks and hoots.

Medieval horn

Musicians blow air through the tubes of differently shaped wind instruments to produce sounds, from low rumbles, to high whistling notes. Hadrosaurs may have made similar sounds, and the dinosaur world was probably quite noisy.

# DINOSAUR MUMMY

In August 1908, George and Levi Sternberg, brothers from a family of dinosaur hunters, made an amazing discovery in the sandstone hills of Wyoming. They unearthed the first dinosaur mummy ever found – an *Edmontosaurus*, still wrapped in the impression of its skin. Millions of years before, hot weather had dried the dinosaur's body, which was then buried and slowly turned into fossil.

In 1912, near the Red Deer River in Alberta, Canada, Barnum Brown found another important duck-billed specimen – the skin-covered fossil skeleton of a *Corythosaurus*.

**Dinosaur skin to fossil impression**
The carcass of the *Corythosaurus* specimen found by Brown was probably carried away by floods and left stranded on a sandbank in a river. As the waters subsided, deep layers of sand and silt settled on top of the dead dinosaur.

The dinosaur carcass was not eaten by scavengers. The soft insides probably rotted away, but the bones, tendons, and tough skin survived long enough to be preserved as fossil.

The thick blanket of river sand and silt that covered the dinosaur carcass kept the pattern and texture of its skin intact long enough to leave an impression on the rocks that formed around it.

## Cousin of *Corythosaurus*

*Edmontosaurus* was another member of the duck-billed, or hadrosaur, family. Unlike *Corythosaurus,* it had a flat skull but may have had an inflatable pouch of skin over its snout to make calling sounds. *Edmontosaurus* lived slightly later than *Corythosaurus* in the same area, now known as North America, and was one of the last surviving dinosaurs.

The dinosaur's soft flesh rotted away, leaving a perfect imprint in the surrounding rock. Over millions of years, chemicals in the hardening sand and silt slowly turned the buried *Corythosaurus* bones into stony fossils.

## *Edmontosaurus* fossil mummy

The mummified *Edmontosaurus* was found by the Sternberg family in Niobrara County, Wyoming. It gave scientists the first evidence that dinosaur skin was similar to that of living reptiles. This specimen is now on display at the AMNH.

## Skin print

This fossilized impression, found by Barnum Brown, clearly shows that *Corythosaurus* skin was covered in a mosaic of small, pebbly bumps. But it cannot tell us what color the markings on the dinosaur's body may have been.

Dry heat made the tendons of the *Edmontosaurus* carcass shrink. The body twisted, with its legs and ribs in the air, and its head pulled back behind the shoulders.

# RIVERSIDE FEAST

About 75 million years ago, *Corythosaurus* foraged along a broad, flat plain crisscrossed by swamps and rivers. This plain lay along the western shores of a great sea that washed from north to south across the middle of the land that is now called North America.

Many other plant-eating and meat-eating dinosaurs roamed through the vast forests with *Corythosaurus*. The plant-eaters fed on ferns and trees including conifers, cypresses, and flowering magnolias, which flourished amidst the waterlogged swamps and river channels.

**Dinosaur heaven**
The lush forests and rivers attracted many kinds of dinosaurs. Numerous plants grew to feed the herds of hungry herbivores, and there was a large supply of fresh water to drink. Lone meat-eaters, or carnivores, such as *Albertosaurus*, prowled the area, hoping to catch a young or sickly plant-eater.

**Watching out for danger**
*Corythosaurus* may have had excellent senses of sight, smell, and hearing. At the first sign of danger from a predator, it could sound the alarm with a booming, loud hoot from its high, crested head.

**Running away**
*Corythosaurus* enjoyed a diet of palm leaves, pine needles, fruits, and seeds. But at the first sign of a predator, it would quickly end its feast and rise up on its hind legs to escape.

Duckbills may have paddled through the rivers and swamps, feeding on overhanging branches. Sometimes, the water may have been the only place to escape from an attacking predator.

After the hadrosaurs, the horned dinosaurs were the second largest group by the riverside. Single-horned *Centrosaurus* could defend itself against attack with its sharp horns.

Away from the riverbank, a group of *Lambeosaurus* would have watched nervously for the approach of a prowling *Albertosaurus*.

### Ferocious hunter
Fierce *Albertosaurus* hunted by the river. Its razor-sharp teeth could slash the soft flesh of its victims, the plant-eaters.

*Euoplocephalus* was well armored against *Albertosaurus*.

### Group defense
*Chasmosaurus* used its long, sharp brow horns in defense against an *Albertosaurus*. In times of danger, a herd of *Chasmosaurus* might have formed a circle for protection and turned, horns outward, to face their attacker.

### Poor swimmer
In the past, researchers believed that *Corythosaurus* could swim by waving its tail to and fro in the water, like a crocodile. Fossil evidence shows that a cage of bony rods held its back and tail rigid so that it could not swim. In fact, *Corythosaurus* could only paddle in shallow river waters.

A young *Corythosaurus* prepares to run for its life.

# CORYTHOSAURUS SPECIMEN AND FAMILY FACTS

- **Specimen number:** AMNH 5338
- **Excavated by:** Barnum Brown
- **Excavation:** 1914, along the Red Deer River, near Steveville, Alberta, Canada
- **Bones found:** Almost complete skeleton, except for some hand and finger bones. Only about one-third of tail bones found
- **Where displayed:** American Museum of Natural History, New York City
- **Constructed:** Mounted as a half skeleton at the AMNH, and displayed in its original resting burial position. Plaster and glue used to repair and strengthen

## 🏛 ON THE MUSEUM TRAIL 🏛

### A museum guide to hadrosaurid specimens
A partial listing of both fossils and replica casts of fossils.

**UNITED STATES**
(*Edmontosaurus, Maiasaura, Parasaurolophus*) University of California Museum of Paleontology, Berkeley, California
(*Maiasaura*) Museum of the Rockies, Bozeman, Montana
(*Lambeosaurus*) Field Museum of Natural History, Chicago, Illinois
(*Corythosaurus, Edmontosaurus, Lambeosaurus, Saurolophus*) American Museum of Natural History, New York
(*Corythosaurus, Edmontosaurus*) National Museum of Natural History, Smithsonian Institution, Washington, D.C.

**CANADA**
(*Corythosaurus, Edmontosaurus, Kritosaurus, Lambeosaurus, Parasaurolophus, Prosaurolophus*) Royal Ontario Museum, Toronto, Ontario
(*Corythosaurus, Hadrosaurus, Hypacrosaurus, Lambeosaurus, Maiasaura, Prosaurolophus*) Tyrrell Museum of Paleontology, Drumheller, Alberta

Hadrosaurid specimens may also be found in museums in Argentina, China, France, Germany, Japan, Mongolia, Poland, Russia, Sweden, Taiwan, and the United Kingdom.

**Cased dinosaur**
*Corythosaurus* is displayed at the AMNH in its original death pose.

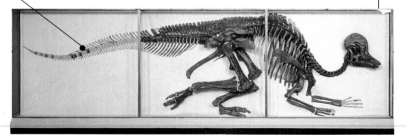

*Corythosaurus* had a strange helmeted head. It lived about 75 million years ago in North America.

## Around the world

Hadrosaurid dinosaurs have been found in North and South America, Europe, and Asia. They lived as far north as Alaska and as far south as Argentina. This map shows where some members of the hadrosaur family have been found.

### Key to map

1  *Corythosaurus*
2  *Edmontosaurus*
3  *Kritosaurus*
4  *Lambeosaurus*
5  *Parasaurolophus*
6  *Saurolophus*

## Family members

*Corythosaurus* is a member of the hadrosaur family, or duck-billed dinosaurs. These were all members of a larger group called the ornithopods.

*Parasaurolophus* lived at about the same time as *Corythosaurus* and in the same areas.

*Lambeosaurus* was larger than *Corythosaurus* and also lived at the same time and in the same parts of North America.

*Saurolophus* had a spiked head crest and, unlike *Corythosaurus*, lived in Asia as well as in North America. It lived a little later in time.

Flat-headed *Edmontosaurus* is one of the most common fossil finds among hadrosaurs. It lived later in time than *Corythosaurus* and was one of the last duck-bills living in North America. It was over 49 ft in length (13 m).

*Kritosaurus* was over 29 ft long (9 m). It had one of the simplest head shapes of the hadrosaurs. Only a bump in front of its eyes stood out on its flat head.

69

# TRICERATOPS

*Triceratops* was one of the last dinosaurs to walk the Earth. It lived at the end of the Cretaceous Period and shared its world with *Tyrannosaurus rex*, the ferocious meat-eater. Did the large, bony head-frill and long horns of *Triceratops* protect it from this terrifying attacker? Possibly, but we do not know for sure. *Triceratops* and other horned dinosaurs, or ceratopsids, have different shapes and sizes of horns and frills. It seems most likely that the horns were used for defense, and the large frills for display.

The shape of the horns and head frills varies a lot between different individual *Triceratops*. The horns above the eyes are sometimes curved forwards and sometimes straight, and some frills are flatter than others. Until recently, scientists divided *Triceratops* into thirteen different species based on these differences. Now it has been recognized that there is one or maybe two species of *Triceratops*. The shapes and sizes of horns and frills vary between individuals in the same way that some of our features do, too.

*Triceratops* and other horned dinosaurs were plant-eaters with sharp beaks and scissor-like teeth. Like many plant-eaters, they lived in herds. One fossil site in Canada has revealed the remains of a herd of more than 1,000 horned dinosaur babies and adults that were washed away while trying to cross a flooded river. Similar accidents happen to plant-eating herds such as caribou and wildebeest today, just as they did to horned dinosaurs all those millions of years ago.

# THREE-HORNED FACE

*Triceratops*, with its huge horns and bony head-frill, was one of the last surviving dinosaurs. Sixty-five million years after its death, scientists are able to piece together information gathered from clues left behind, and learn how this dinosaur lived. *Triceratops* is one of the most common dinosaurs to be found in western North America. Fossil hunters have collected the remains of more than 1,500 *Triceratops* – although few of these are complete skeletons. Finding a complete skeleton of any dinosaur, even of a common one, such as *Triceratops*, is a rare and thrilling event.

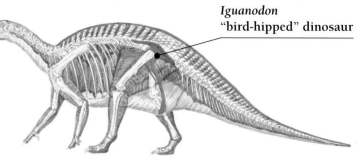

*Iguanodon* "bird-hipped" dinosaur

**Horned family**
*Triceratops* belongs to the group of horned dinosaurs called the ceratopsids. Their large horns and strong bodies were a good defense against predators.

*Triceratops* (try-ser-rah-tops) means "three-horned face."

**Bird-hipped**
*Triceratops* was a "bird-hipped" or ornithischian dinosaur. The two lower bones of its pelvis pointed backwards and down.

*Triceratops* had a huge, frilled crest that extended from the back of its skull and doubled the size of its head.

*Triceratops* was armed with long, stabbing nose and eyebrow horns.

## Changing Earth

*Triceratops* lived right at the end of the Cretaceous Period, at the same time as the ferocious *Tyrannosaurus rex*.

| TRIASSIC PERIOD | JURASSIC PERIOD | CRETACEOUS PERIOD |
|---|---|---|
| 248–205 million years ago | 205–144 million years ago | 144–65 million years ago |

The frills of some *Triceratops* have holes punched right through the bone. It has been suggested that these may be punctures made by the horn tips during combat with other *Triceratops*.

### Plant-eater

Like other ceratopsids, *Triceratops* was a plant-eater, or herbivore. It had a sharp, toothless beak to slice through tough leaves and twigs.

*Triceratops* weighed as much as a fully grown African elephant. Its great bulk was supported by four sturdy legs.

FACT FILE
- **Lived:** 67-65 million years ago, during the Late Cretaceous Period
- **Family:** Ceratopsids, the horned dinosaurs
- **Dinosaur type:** Bird-hipped (ornithischian)
- **Diet:** Plants
- **Weight when alive:** Over 6 tons (6 tonnes)
- **Height:** Over 9 ft (3 m)
- **Length:** Over 29 ft (up to 9 m)
- **Top speed:** 15 mph (about 25 km/h)

# BURIED TREASURE

Only the skull survives of one *Triceratops* that died about 65 million years ago. The rest of the bones may have been eaten by animals or swept away by floods. The skull was buried in the mud and sand of a riverbed, where it was slowly turned into stony fossil.

The skull was discovered in 1909 at Seven Mile Creek, Niobrara County, Wyoming, by the American fossil hunter, George Sternberg, and his family. Parts of another *Triceratops* were found in the same year by Barnum Brown in Hell Creek, Montana.

**Fossil world**
The *Triceratops* skull found in 1909 is the only part left of this dinosaur that lived about 65 million years ago. The skull was slowly turned as hard as stone by chemicals in the rock where it lay buried.

**1 Living dinosaur**
About 65 million years ago, *Triceratops* sips water from a rushing river. The river flows past prehistoric trees and plants such as monkey puzzles, willows, conifers, palms, and ferns.

**2 Bare bones**
A few years later, *Triceratops* has died from old age or disease. Its bones have been picked clean by scavengers and now lie on the bank of a dried-up riverbed.

**3 Buried skull**
*Triceratops'* skull lies buried in the mud and sand of the riverbed. The rest of the skeleton has been destroyed by animals, plants, and the weather.

---

## DINOSAUR DETECTIVE
### George Sternberg (1883 – 1969)

George Sternberg was the eldest of Charles Sternberg's three sons. He was first taken fossil collecting at the age of six and continued to work on fossils for another 66 years. With his father and brothers, George Sternberg discovered some of the most amazing fossil treasures ever found in North America.

| | |
|---|---|
| 1883 | *Born in Lawrence, Kansas.* |
| 1908 | *Discovered with his brother Levi the first known fossil of a mummified dinosaur, a duckbill named* **Edmontosaurus.** |
| 1909 | *Discovered with his father and brothers a fine skull of* **Triceratops.** |
| 1952 | *Discovered the fossil of a 14 ft (4 m) long prehistoric fish, containing a fish almost 6 ft (2 m) long that it had eaten before it died.* |
| 1969 | *Died at age 86 on October 23 in Hays, Kansas.* |
| 1970 | *The fossil collection at Fort Hays State University, Kansas, founded by George Sternberg, was officially designated the Sternberg Museum.* |

*Friendly fossil hunters*
*The Sternbergs, on a fossil-collecting expedition, visit their fellow dinosaur hunter Barnum Brown.*

## Bone and horn

Now preserved as a hard, stony fossil, the brow horn of *Triceratops* was once living bone. During the animal's lifetime, the bone was encased in a layer of horn, ending in a sharp tip. Grooves in the surface of the fossil show where the bone was once fed by a pattern of blood vessels.

## Tracing *Triceratops*

Remains of *Triceratops* have been found in several sites in North America, in rocks formed during the Cretaceous Period of the Earth's history. Barnum Brown discovered his specimens near Hell Creek, Montana, while the Sternbergs' skull came from farther south, along a riverside in Niobrara County, Wyoming. Many of the best fossil specimens of *Triceratops* have come from this area.

Seven Mile Creek, Wyoming

Discovery site of the *Triceratops* skull

## 6 Fossil find

Centuries of wind and rain have worn the rocks of the ancient riverbed into barren hills and steep-sided canyons. The weather has also exposed parts of the *Triceratops* skull, which now lies waiting to be discovered.

## 4 Stony fossil

15 million years after the death of *Triceratops*, the dinosaurs have died out and mammals have taken over the Earth. Chemicals have slowly turned the mud and sand of the old riverbed into rock, and the buried skull into hard, stony fossil.

## 5 Icy grave

15,000 years ago, the land lies frozen in an Ice Age. Earth movements have pushed up the fossil skull in its rocky layer, along with a new range of mountains.

# FOSSIL FRAGMENTS

In 1909, the Sternberg family was hunting fossils on behalf of the American Museum of Natural History (AMNH) in New York. The Sternbergs found a fine example of a *Triceratops* skull in the barren hills of Wyoming. They cleared away tons of rock to expose the ancient dinosaur remains.

The fossils were packed up and shipped to New York. At the AMNH, scientists carefully restored the *Triceratops* skull. The skull was then mounted, together with remains from at least four different *Triceratops* animals, to create a freestanding fossil skeleton for display in the Museum's world-famous dinosaur hall.

Charles Sternberg chisels out the skull of a horned dinosaur.

### 2 Fossil discovery
In 1909, George Sternberg noticed fossil fragments emerging from a steep hillside. He and his brothers began to chip away the stone around the fragile dinosaur bones, using hammers, picks, and chisels.
The Sternbergs slowly uncovered the shattered remains of a *Triceratops* skull.

### 1 Barren hunting ground
The Sternbergs traveled to Wyoming to hunt fossils in the rugged badlands, where ancient rocks had weathered into flat-topped hills and steep-sided canyons. The dinosaur hunters looked for fragments of fossil, clues to greater treasures buried in the hillsides.

The *Triceratops* skull was found lying upside down.

### 3 Dinosaur graveyard
One year earlier, the Sternbergs had uncovered fossil remains of another *Triceratops* in the same area as their new find. The sandstone rock layers of Wyoming proved to be a dinosaur graveyard, rich in fossil treasures.

### 4 Surviving skull
Only the *Triceratops* skull had survived as a fossil. The other dinosaur bones had been destroyed before they could be buried. Once the Sternbergs had cleared the rock away from the fossil, they sifted the debris to find any missing pieces of the badly broken frill.

### 5 Plaster jackets
The fragile fossil bones needed to be well protected in transit to the AMNH. First, the fossils were covered in a protective layer of thin paper. Next, the bones were wrapped in burlap soaked in plaster.

The supportive plaster jacket held the shattered fossil bones together.

### 6 Heavy load
When the plaster was dry, the heavy blocks containing the sections of skull were hoisted into strong wooden crates. At last the *Triceratops* skull was ready to begin its long journey to New York.

Glue and plaster were used to mend the cracked fossils.

### 7 Horse and cart
Horses were used to drag the wooden crates out of the fossil quarry. At the top of the slope, the boxes were loaded on to a horse-drawn cart and dragged across the rough countryside to the nearest railroad station.

### 8 Skull restoration
Back at the AMNH, scientists needed great skill to repair the skull because the shattered frill had to be rebuilt from many pieces. The *Triceratops* skull was supported on a metal rod and wooden props while workers slowly pieced it together.

The small, bony knobs from along the edge of the frill were not found and were not replaced.

# SKULL AND BONES

After several years of preparation, the *Triceratops* skull found by the Sternbergs and the skeleton found by Barnum Brown were finally ready for display at the American Museum of Natural History. One of the strongest dinosaurs, *Triceratops* with its massive horned skull and nearly 29 ft-long (over 9 m), barrel-like body, was built to withstand attack from the fiercest predator. Some scientists believe that *Triceratops* could have charged at almost 15 mph (more than 25 km/h) in defense against an attacking meat-eater.

**Crash protector**
The thick skull and strongly built neck and hips of *Triceratops* all helped it to withstand impact when it crashed into an attacker or locked horns with a rival. *Triceratops* could also charge quickly over short distances on its powerful legs. It would not have been easy prey, even for the huge meat-eating dinosaurs such as *Tyrannosaurus rex.*

Skin-covered bony
frill edged with a
rim of bony studs

Brow horn, over 3 ft
(about 1 m) long

Short
nose horn

Eyes were set in deep,
well-protected sockets

**Huge head**
The enormous head of *Triceratops* made up almost one-third of its overall length. The head was armed with long, sharp, bone-filled horns on the brow and nose. The head-frill was edged with bony lumps and protected the dinosaur's powerful neck. The horns would have been longer in life, before the outer layer decayed.

Powerful jaws
were operated
by huge muscles
stretching down
from the frill.

Row of teeth for
grinding food

Humerus (upper
armbones)

Ulna and radius
(forearm bones)

**Front and back view**
The high, wide frill and long horns added to the threatening size of *Triceratops'* head. Massive strong legs gave *Triceratops* great strength when facing an attacker.

The horns could be used as powerful weapons if they did not scare off an attacker.

Ten back vertebrae gave strength and rigidity to the pelvis.

The sharp-edged, horny beak was used to snip off tough leaves and branches.

Back vertebrae

**Tail position**
Dinosaurs probably walked with their tails held above the ground. Dinosaur footprints left fossilized in mud show no marks left by dragging tails. In the past, however, scientists often mounted skeletons with tails brushing the ground.

Pubis (lower pelvic bone)

The ischium (upper pelvic bone) anchored the leg muscles, while the lower pelvic bones supported and protected the soft internal organs.

Long, curved ribs gave *Triceratops* a deep-chested, stocky body.

There were probably over 30 vertebrae in the tail of *Triceratops*.

Femur (thigh bone)

Tibia (shin bone)

Short front legs and longer rear legs were powerful bone pillars.

Four broad toes on the rear feet and five toes on the front feet ended in hooflike claws that helped spread the great weight of *Triceratops*.

Fibula (leg bone)

# HUNGRY HERDERS

Triceratops was one of the most common dinosaurs living 65 million years ago in the area now known as North America. Huge herds of horned plant-eaters roamed through the forests and along the banks of rivers and the edges of swamps. The hordes of hungry dinosaurs fed on trees, shrubs, and ferns. Only tall plants were safe from the giant appetite of Triceratops.

**Flowering food**
Triceratops and the other plant-eaters of the time ate the new flowering plants, such as magnolia, oak, and laurel, that appeared during the Cretaceous Period.

**Snipping beak**
Triceratops used its sharp beak to snip off leaves and twigs that grew up to 9 ft (3 m) from the ground.

**Growing beak**
Triceratops' beak was worn down by its rough diet but may have continued to grow throughout the dinosaur's lifetime, like human fingernails.

**Herbivores and hunters**
Many dinosaurs fed on the plants that grew on the lush plains. Fierce meat-eaters followed the herds, hunting young or sickly herbivores.

**Edmontosaurus**
The duck-billed dinosaur *Edmontosaurus* lived in a herd. It could reach leaves on tree branches that were out of *Triceratops*' reach.

**Pachycephalosaurus**
*Pachycephalosaurus* had a thick, domed head, ringed by bony spikes, that gave no protection against a predator.

**Tyrannosaurus and Ornithomimus**
*Triceratops* had dangerously sharp horns to defend itself against fierce *Tyrannosaurus*. *Ornithomimus* was built like a modern-day ostrich and could have run away from any danger.

Triceratops

Tyrannosaurus

Ornithomimus

**Torosaurus**
*Torosaurus* had a huge, horned skull. It was always on the lookout for danger from an attacking predator.

**Migration**
*Triceratops* could only survive if it found enough to eat. During a drought, *Triceratops* and the other plant-eaters may have migrated long distances in search of new feeding grounds.

**Jaws like shears**
*Triceratops*' tooth-lined jaws worked like garden shears to slice up plants. The flat surface on the teeth worked like a grindstone.

# HORNED DEFENSE

Triceratops was well protected against the fierce predators, such as *Tyrannosaurus*, that tracked the herds of plant-eaters across the great plain. *Triceratops* had long, sharp horns on its forehead and snout and specially strengthened bones in its neck, hip area, and skull to withstand shock if it charged into an attacker. If it were lucky, *Triceratops* would not have to fight at all. The giant bony frill that made its head look so huge might scare off any prowling carnivore, or meat-eater.

**Attacking monster**
A hungry *Tyrannosaurus* spots a *Triceratops* feeding away from its herd. The meat-eater rushes at its prey, hoping to knock it down. It will try to wound *Triceratops* with one fatal bite of its saber-toothed jaws.

**Fighting back**
*Triceratops* shakes its head, bellows, and lunges toward its attacker. Charging forward, *Triceratops* tries to stab the belly of its mighty opponent with its horns. If it succeeds, *Triceratops* may escape from death – this time.

**Standing its ground**
*Triceratops* paws the ground and hisses at *Tyrannosaurus*, looking for a way to escape the terrible hunter's razor-sharp, slashing teeth. But *Tyrannosaurus* is growing tired and may decide to give up and hunt a weaker animal.

## On the move

Standing, walking, or running, *Triceratops* supported its heavy 6 ton (6 tonne) body on strong, stocky legs. The dinosaur may have been capable of short bursts of speed at more than 15 mph (25 km/h).

3 Hip bones take the strain of *Triceratops'* heavy body weight.

1 As *Triceratops* rises from the ground, its long back legs push the hips upward.

2 Huge muscles support *Triceratops'* great body over the front and rear legs.

6 *Triceratops* breaks into a run, perhaps as fast as over 15 mph (25 km/h).

4 *Triceratops* may have walked at speeds of over 6 mph (around 10 km/h).

5 *Triceratops* catches sight of an attacker and prepares to charge.

The rear legs are braced, ready for the impact with *Tyrannosaurus*.

The legs kick up a cloud of dust to try to confuse the attacker.

## Means of defense

*Triceratops* may look a little like a rhinoceros, but it was twice the size and a reptile, not a mammal. Nevertheless, the dinosaur may have defended itself in ways similar to those of a rhino. Some rhinos charge, while others stand in a defensive circle, horns pointing out toward the attacker.

# DESERT ADVENTURES

In 1922, scientists from the American Museum of Natural History first traveled to the Gobi Desert in Mongolia in Central Asia. The expedition had set out to find fossil evidence of early humans. Instead, it was to make one of the most important discoveries ever about dinosaurs. In 1923, the team collected the first known dinosaur eggs and nest, together with fossil bones of *Protoceratops*, the horned dinosaur that was thought to have laid the eggs. Sixty years later, other scientists from the museum returned to the Gobi to find out more about dinosaurs and their young. They discovered the dinosaur nests and eggs belonged to a completely different dinosaur, *Oviraptor*.

**Making maps**
The team's geologist, Frederick K. Morris, drew up detailed maps. These were used to understand the history of the rocks in which the dinosaur fossils were found and to help the team to find their way across the desert.

Site of discovery of the dinosaur eggs, nest, and *Protoceratops* bones

Russian Federation

"Flaming Cliffs" of Bayn Dzak, Gobi Desert, Mongolia

China

India

**Dinosaur hunter**
Walter Granger was deputy leader on the AMNH expeditions to the Gobi, as well as the chief paleontologist. Granger is seen here, delicately brushing sand and grit from a fossil.

**Finding the eggs**
On July 13, 1923, the assistant, George Olsen, came across three shattered fossil eggs and some dinosaur bones. Andrews and Granger realized that the team had discovered real proof that dinosaurs hatched from eggs, like other reptiles.

**Expedition leader**
Roy Chapman Andrews was the leader of the 1923 expedition. He had begun raising funds and planning the expedition several years earlier.

**Cars and camels**
Mongolian and Chinese scientists joined the American team on their five expeditions to the Gobi Desert in the 1920s. They traveled in large cars and met camel trains regularly to receive fresh supplies of food and gas.

## Asian cousin of *Triceratops*

*Protoceratops* was only 3 ft to over 8 ft long (1 m to 2.5 m), about the size of a small horse. *Protoceratops* lived about 85 million years ago, on the continent now called Asia. Its relatives, the horned dinosaurs, such as *Triceratops*, have mainly been found in North America.

*Protoceratops* had a beak, short frill, and wide cheekbones. It had no horns, even though it was a member of the family of horned dinosaurs.

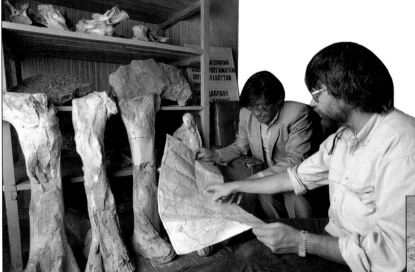

### 1 Planning an expedition

Since the late 1980s, scientists from the AMNH have returned several times to the Gobi Desert. Before each trip, they check weather patterns and plan routes and exploration sites with Mongolian colleagues, to allow as much time as possible for collecting fossils.

### 2 Searching for clues

The field leader, Mark Norell, studies debris on the dry desert floor. Fossils look shinier than the red sand and mudstone. Norell studies the fossils to decide whether it would be worth spending time searching for dinosaur remains in this area.

### 3 Collecting samples

A scientist collects samples of dinosaur bone from the crumbling, rocky cliffs. During the day, the desert is baking hot. At night, it can be freezing cold. Few plants grow here, and any rocks and bones exposed to the heat and cold are soon worn into dust.

### 4 Excavating fossils

The scientists work slowly to brush away the sand from around a dinosaur skull. They chip away any hard lumps of rock with small picks. The exposed fossil is then strengthened with a coating of glue.

### 5 Packing up the fossils

Once the glue is dry, each fossil is wrapped in a thin lining of paper, followed by burlap soaked in plaster. When the protective plaster layer has set hard, the fossil can be lifted and carried back to camp, ready to be shipped back for study at the AMNH.

# DINOSAUR BABIES

Since the discovery of fossil dinosaur eggs, nests, and bones in the Gobi Desert in 1923, similar finds have been made around the world. Scientists have been able to use these remains to work out how dinosaurs may have developed, and how they tended their young. Most of the Gobi nests are now known to belong to *Oviraptor,* but perhaps *Protoceratops* nested in a similar way.

The many *Protoceratops* skeletons found range from tiny skeletons to fully grown adults. These bones show how *Protoceratops* changed in size and shape as it grew.

All these findings may offer clues to the lives of *Triceratops* and other horned dinosaurs, whose nests, eggs, and babies have not yet been found.

**Nesting sites**
It is thought that *Protoceratops* probably scooped out a bowl-shaped nest in soft, dry sand – laying its eggs in a circle as it turned around in the nest. Many females may have nested at a single site – a large number of adults staying close together perhaps helped to keep predators away.

Like a modern-day reptile, a dinosaur would have laid its eggs from an opening under its tail, just behind the hip bones.

It was once thought that an adult *Protoceratops* may have had to protect its eggs from nest-robbing dinosaurs such as *Oviraptor.* However, work by the AMNH scientists in the 1990's has shown that *Oviraptor* did not rob *Protoceratops'* nests. Adult *Oviraptor* have been found sitting on their own clutches of eggs – once thought to belong to *Protoceratops.*

**Hatching out**
The baby *Protoceratops* cracked their eggs open from the inside. They may have used their tiny beaks to break through the shell or burst through by flexing their muscles hard.

**Feeding the young**
Soon after hatching, the baby *Protoceratops* would have stretched their legs and set off in search of food. The adults may have stayed close by to bring plants to the nest for the first few days.

Short frill

### Shell fragments
Most reptiles lay eggs with soft shells, but dinosaur shells were hard. Some shells had very fine lines or bumps. The babies probably left the nest soon after hatching and did not trample the shells underfoot, leaving them in large pieces.

The reconstructed skeleton of an adult *Protoceratops* with a small bump on the snout.

### Growing up
Many *Protoceratops* skulls have been found. These show how the dinosaurs' skulls and jaws developed at different stages in growth, from hatching to adulthood.

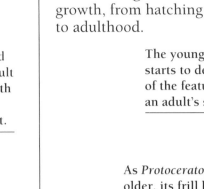

The skull of a newly hatched *Protoceratops*.

A *Protoceratops* baby has large eye sockets set in a small skull.

The young *Protoceratops* starts to develop more of the features of an adult's skull.

As *Protoceratops* grows older, its frill becomes larger and wider.

Male and female *Protoceratops* may have developed different characteristics. This may be a male, with a wide frill and a smooth snout.

The growing frill anchors *Protoceratops'* large jaw muscles. This gives the jaw the strength to slice through tough leaves and stems.

*Protoceratops* is almost fully grown. Its beak and snout have become narrower, and the back of the skull is wider.

*Protoceratops* is now a fully developed adult. Its wide cheekbones and frill stand out from the skull.

### Nest arrangement
One fossil nest contained a clutch of 18 eggs – five eggs laid in the middle, with 11 more laid in a circle around these, and two more eggs on the outside. At one time nests like these were thought to belong to *Protoceratops'* but the discovery of an *Oviraptor* embryo inside this kind of egg in 1995 overturned 70 years of misidentification.

Reptiles today, such as this baby snake, hatch out of a soft-skinned, leathery egg.

Cracked fossil eggs, about 12 in (30 cm) long, stand up in the sand, where they were laid about 85 million years ago.

# HEAD-FRILLS AND HORNS

Spikes, lumps, fans, and frills decorated the heads of the family of horned dinosaurs, the ceratopsids. Differences in the shape and size of skulls may have helped the living dinosaurs to recognize one another and indicated whether an animal was male or female, young or old. Head features help scientists to distinguish one horned dinosaur from another, because few well-preserved total skeletons have been found.

In addition to providing armor against an attacking predator, the horns of this dinosaur family probably had another purpose. Just as deer lock antlers today, the ceratopsid dinosaurs may have used their horns against rivals to win territory or a mate.

Some scientists believe that the head-frills and spikes of the living dinosaurs may have been highly colored as a warning to predators or to attract a mate, but no fossil evidence survives to support this theory.

Large "windows" made the frill lighter, helping *Chasmosaurus* to more easily lift its huge head.

*Chasmosaurus*

**Chasmosaurus**
Small spikes lined the rear and side edges of *Chasmosaurus'* frill.

Short frill

Sharp, toothless beak

Stout nose horn

Eye socket

*Centrosaurus*

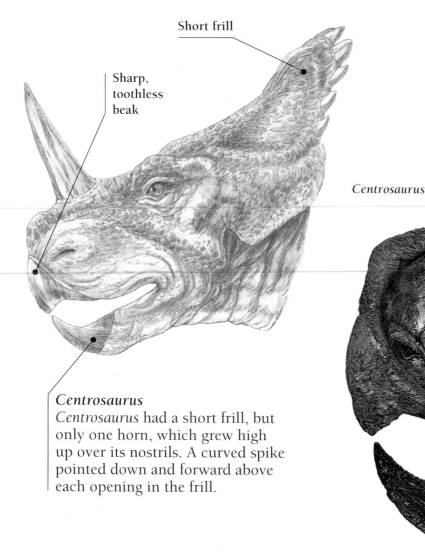

**Centrosaurus**
*Centrosaurus* had a short frill, but only one horn, which grew high up over its nostrils. A curved spike pointed down and forward above each opening in the frill.

The massive jaw muscles bulged through spaces in the side of the frill when *Centrosaurus* closed its jaws.

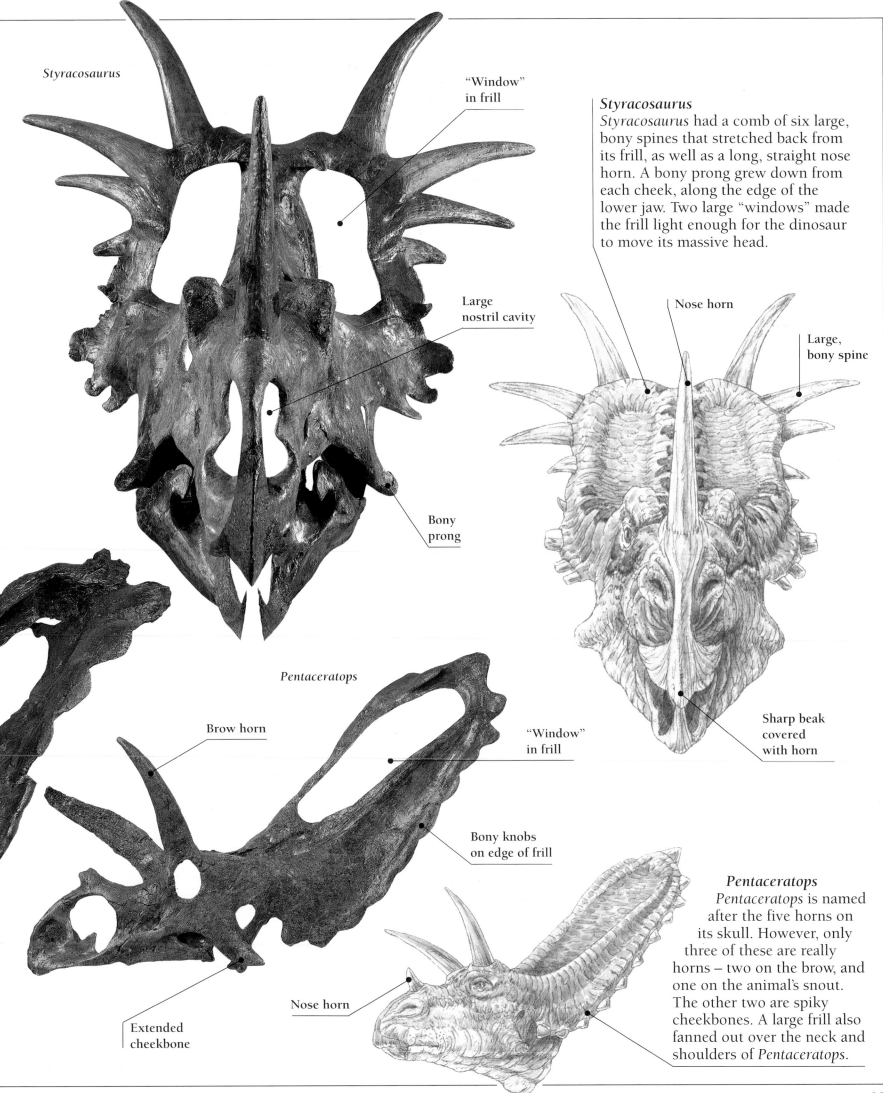

*Styracosaurus*

"Window" in frill

### Styracosaurus
*Styracosaurus* had a comb of six large, bony spines that stretched back from its frill, as well as a long, straight nose horn. A bony prong grew down from each cheek, along the edge of the lower jaw. Two large "windows" made the frill light enough for the dinosaur to move its massive head.

Large nostril cavity

Bony prong

Nose horn

Large, bony spine

Sharp beak covered with horn

*Pentaceratops*

Brow horn

"Window" in frill

Bony knobs on edge of frill

Nose horn

Extended cheekbone

### Pentaceratops
*Pentaceratops* is named after the five horns on its skull. However, only three of these are really horns – two on the brow, and one on the animal's snout. The other two are spiky cheekbones. A large frill also fanned out over the neck and shoulders of *Pentaceratops*.

# TRICERATOPS SPECIMEN AND FAMILY FACTS

- **Specimen numbers:** AMNH 5116, 5033, 5039, 5045
- **Excavated by:** The Sternberg family; Barnum Brown
- **Excavation:** Seven Mile Creek, Niobrara County, Wyoming; Hell Creek, Montana

- **Bones found:** Skull and most of the skeleton, except for the front limbs; composite skeleton is made up of the remains of at least four separate animals
- **Where displayed:** American Museum of Natural History, New York City

## 🏛 ON THE MUSEUM TRAIL 🏛

### A museum guide to Ceratopsid specimens
A partial listing of both fossils and replica casts of fossils.

**CANADA**
(*Monoclonius, Styracosaurus, Triceratops*) National Museum of Natural Sciences, Ottawa, Ontario
(*Chasmosaurus*) Royal Ontario Museum, Toronto, Ontario
(*Centrosaurus, Chasmosaurus, Triceratops*) Tyrrell Museum of Paleontology, Drumheller, Alberta

**UNITED KINGDOM**
(*Centrosaurus, Protoceratops, Triceratops*) The Natural History Museum, London

**U.S.**
(*Protoceratops*) Carnegie Museum of Natural History, Pittsburgh, Pennsylvania
(*Centrosaurus, Triceratops*) National Museum of Natural History, Smithsonian Institution, Washington, D.C.
(*Centrosaurus, Torosaurus*) Peabody Museum of Natural History, Yale University, New Haven, Connecticut
(*Triceratops*) Pratt Museum (Amherst College), Amherst, Massachusetts
(*Triceratops*) The Science Museum of Minnesota, St. Paul, Minnesota
(*Triceratops*) University of Nebraska State Museum, Lincoln, Nebraska

Ceratopsid specimens may also be found in museums in China, France, Germany, Japan, Mongolia, Poland, Russia, Spain, and Sweden.

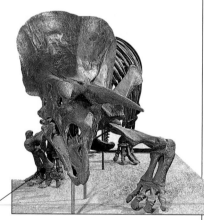

The *Triceratops* skeleton on display at the AMNH was made up from the fossil remains of at least four different animals.

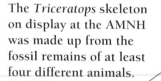

*Triceratops* was one of the last dinosaurs on Earth. Its huge horns and giant frill made this large dinosaur look even bigger.

## Changing world

This map shows areas in which horned dinosaurs have been discovered. Although *Triceratops* is one of the most common dinosaurs to be found, its remains and those of other horned dinosaurs have been found only on the continents of North America and Asia.

### Key to map

1 *Chasmosaurus*
2 *Centrosaurus*
3 *Pentaceratops*
4 *Styracosaurus*
5 *Torosaurus*
6 *Triceratops*
7 *Protoceratops*

## The horned dinosaur family

*Triceratops* was a member of the chasmosaurines, one of two groups of horned dinosaurs. The other group, the centrosaurines, had shorter head frills and longer nose horns. Together they belonged to the ceratopsid family.

*Torosaurus* had the largest skull of the horned dinosaurs, but fossil remains of its limbs and body have not yet been found. *Torosaurus* also lived in the Cretaceous Period and in the same part of the world as *Triceratops*.

A long-frilled horned dinosaur, *Pentaceratops* was about the same size as *Triceratops*. It became extinct just before *Triceratops* appeared.

*Chasmosaurus* lived about 75 million years ago. Its fossil remains have been found in Alberta, Canada, and Texas.

*Centrosaurus* was over 18 ft (5 m) long and lived 75 million years ago in the land that is now known as North America.

*Styracosaurus* had long horns and a short frill. It lived earlier than *Triceratops* and, like most horned dinosaurs, has been found in North America.

*Protoceratops* is the only horned dinosaur yet to be found in Central Asia. It was the size of a small horse.

# GLOSSARY

**carcass**
The body of a dead animal.

**carnivore**
A meat-eating animal.

**carnosaur**
A group of dinosaurs that were the largest meat-eaters to have lived on land.

**cast**
A replica of a fossil, made from a mold of the original.

**ceratopsids**
Family of horned dinosaurs. There were two groups of ceratopsids: the chasmosaurines and the centrosaurines. *Triceratops* was a member of the chasmosaurines.

**composite skeleton**
A skeleton made up of parts from more than one incomplete specimen.

**crest**
A decoration of feathers, skin, or bone growing on top of an animal's head; used by an animal to signal to other animals of its kind.

**Cretaceous Period**
Part of the Earth's history which lasted from 144 million years ago until the dinosaurs died out 65 million years ago. *Tyrannosaurus rex* lived during this period.

**dinosaurs**
A group of extinct, land-living reptiles that lived on Earth from 230 to 65 million years ago.

**duck-billed dinosaur**
Another name for a hadrosaur, a dinosaur with a duck-like beak.

**environment**
The land, water, and climate that surrounds living things and affects how they live.

**excavate**
To dig up an object such as a fossil.

**extinction**
When living things, such as dinosaurs, die out and disappear from the Earth forever.

**formation**
A group of rock layers that are recognizable from one place to another.

**fossil**
Part of a dead plant or animal that has been buried and turned as hard as stone by chemicals in the rock.

**gastrolith**
A stone swallowed by a dinosaur and used in part of its stomach to help grind up tough plants.

**glass fiber**
A fine mat of glass threads that is used to strengthen plastic used for fossil casts.

**hadrosaur**
Another name for a duck-billed dinosaur, such as *Corythosaurus*.

**head frill**
The wide rim of bone that fans out from the back of the skull of a horned dinosaur.

**herbivore**
A plant-eating animal.

**horns**
Sharp, pointed features that grew on the skulls of horned dinosaurs. They were made of material like that of human fingernails, growing over a bony core.

**impression**
A copy of the shape of a fossil and the marks on its surface.

**Jurassic Period**
Part of the Earth's history from 205 to 144 million years ago, when large plant-eating sauropod dinosaurs were common.

**mammal**
An animal that has hair-covered skin, gives birth to live young, and feeds them with milk.

**mosaic**
A pattern made up of small lumps or pieces.

**mold**
The impression of an original object from which a cast is made.

**mummy**
A carcass that has been dried out by natural or chemical means before being buried, and so preserved from rotting.

**organ**
A soft part inside an animal's body, such as the heart or stomach.

**ornithischian dinosaur**
The bird-hipped type of dinosaur, in which both lower hip bones point down and backwards.

**ornithopods**
A group of plant-eating dinosaurs that normally walked on two legs.

**paleontologist**
A scientist who studies fossils and life in ancient times.

**pelvis**
The group of bones where the legs join the backbone of an animal's skeleton.

**predator**
An animal that hunts and kills other animals to eat.

**reptile**
A scaly animal that lays shelled eggs, such as the turtles, snakes, lizards, and crocodiles of today. Dinosaurs were reptiles.

**saurischian dinosaur**
The lizard-hipped type of dinosaur with one of the two lower hip bones pointing down and forwards and the other bone pointing down and backwards.

**sauropod**
A group of large, plant-eating, lizard-hipped dinosaurs, one of which was *Barosaurus*.

**scavenger**
A meat-eater that feeds on prey that is already dead, rather than on prey that it has killed.

**skeleton**
The supporting bony frame inside an animal's body.

**specimen**
One example of a kind of plant or animal, or part of it.

# PRONUNCIATION GUIDE

The following is a guide to pronunciation of the dinosaur names mentioned in this book.

- *Albertosaurus*
  (al-bert-oh-saw-rus)
- *Allosaurus*
  (al-low-saw-rus)
- *Ankylosaurus*
  (ank-kye-low-saw-rus)
- *Apatosaurus*
  (ap-pat-oh-saw-rus)

- *Barosaurus*
  (barrow-saw-rus)
- *Brachiosaurus*
  (brakky-oh-saw-rus)

- *Camarasaurus*
  (kam-ah-ra-saw-rus)
- *Camptosaurus*
  (camp-toe-saw-rus)
- *Centrosaurus*
  (sen-tro-saw-rus)
- *Ceratosaurus*
  (seratto-saw-rus)
- *Cetiosaurus*
  (seaty-oh-saw-rus)
- *Chasmosaurus*
  (kas-mo-saw-rus)
- *Corythosaurus*
  (korrith-oh-saw-rus)

- *Daspletosaurus*
  (dass-pleet-oh-saw-rus)
- *Deinonychus*
  (die-non-uh-cus)
- *Dilophosaurus*
  (dye-loff-oh-saw-rus)
- *Diplodocus*
  (di-plod-ock-us)
- *Dryosaurus*
  (dry-oh-saw-rus)

- *Edmontosaurus*
  (ed-mon-toe-saw-rus)
- *Euoplocephalus*
  (you-oh-plo-keff-allus)

- *Hadrosaurus*
  (had-row-saw-rus)
- *Heterodontosaurus*
  (het-ter-row-dont-oh-saw-rus)
- *Hypacrosaurus*
  (hi-pack-row-saw-rus)

- *Iguanodon*
  (ig-wan-oh-don)

- *Kritosaurus*
  (krit-oh-saw-rus)

- *Lambeosaurus*
  (lam-bay-oh-saw-rus)

- *Maiasaura*
  (my-ah-saw-rah)
- *Mamenchisaurus*
  (mammenkey-saw-rus)
- *Monoclonius*
  (mon-oh-clone-ee-us)
- *Montanoceratops*
  (mon-tan-oh-sera-tops)

- *Ornithomimus*
  (ornith-oh-meem-us)
- *Oviraptor*
  (ovi-rap-tor)

- *Pachycephalosaurus*
  (pakky-seph-ah-low-saw-rus)
- *Parasaurolophus*
  (para-sore-oll-oh-fus)
- *Pentaceratops*
  (pen-tah-ser-ah-tops)
- *Plateosaurus*
  (plat-ay-oh-saw-rus)
- *Prosaurolophus*
  (pro-sore-oll-oh-fus)
- *Protoceratops*
  (pro-toe-sera-tops)

- *Saurolophus*
  (sore-oll-oh-fus)
- *Stegosaurus*
  (stegg-oh-saw-rus)
- *Struthiomimus*
  (strewth-ee-yo-meem-us)
- *Styracosaurus*
  (sty-rack-oh-saw-rus)

- *Tarbosaurus*
  (tar-bow-saw-rus)
- *Torosaurus*
  (tore-oh-saw-rus)
- *Triceratops*
  (try-ser-rah-tops)
- *Troodon*
  (tru-oh-don)
- *Tyrannosaurus rex*
  (tie-ran-oh-saw-rus recks)

**theropods**
All meat-eating lizard-hipped
dinosaurs, such as *Tyrannosaurus rex*.

**Triassic Period**
Part of the Earth's history which
lasted from 248 to 205 million years
ago, during which the dinosaurs
first appeared.

**type specimen**
The one specimen of an animal or
plant that is used as a standard to
compare with other specimens.

**tyrannosaur**
Best-known family within
the carnosaurs.

**vertebrae**
Bones that form the backbone of
animals.

**weathering**
When rocks and soil are broken up
and washed or blown away by wind,
rain, sun, frost, and other features of
the weather.

# INDEX

Numbers in **bold** refer to main entries.

# ACKNOWLEDGMENTS

Picture credits:
t=top, b=bottom, m=middle,
l=left, r=right

### TYRANNOSAURUS REX

Courtesy Department of Library Services, American Museum of Natural History: Neg. no. 37243, 9tr; Neg. no. 335782, 9mr; Neg. no. 18338, 10tl; Neg. no. 18341, 10mr; Neg. no. 121779, 10b; Neg. no. 35923, 11tr.

Model photography by Dave King 1bl, 1mr, 4br, 5, 12ml, 15t, 15br, 16, 17, 19-23.

Museum photography by Lynton Gardiner 11br, 12r, 13, 14br, 15tr, 18ml, 18, 19m, 24mr.

Additional special photography by Paul Bricknell (magnifying glass) 9tl; Andy Crawford 2t, 13bl, 24b; John Down 14r; Philip Dowell (ostrich leg bone); Tim Ridley 10tr; Harry Taylor 8bl; Jerry Young 6tr, 15tl.

### BAROSAURUS

Courtesy Department of Library Services, American Museum of Natural History: Neg. no. 37243, 33mr; The Carnegie Museum of Natural History: Neg. no. 1012, 31br; Special Collections, University of Utah Library: Neg. no. 860, 30bml; Neg. no. 815, 32tl; Neg. no. 763, 32m (upper); Neg. no. 798, 32m (lower); Neg. no. 815, 32bm; Neg. no. 1039, 32br.

Model photography by Dave King 1mr, 2br, 40bl, 42–45, 93br.

Museum photography by Lynton Gardiner 28bl, 28tr, 28mr, 31tl, 32bl, 32tr, 32mr, 33bl, 34–41, 46mr.

Additional special photography by Paul Bricknell (magnifying glass)

31br; Andy Crawford (children) 40, 41, 47; Colin Keates 44mr; Mary Ann Lynch 36tr; Tim Ridley 4tl, 34t, 34mr, 35tl, 46b, 47b.

Barosaurus scale model, 40tr, courtesy of Eugene Gaffney; designed by Shinobu Matsumura; manufactured by Kaiyodo Company Ltd, Japan.

### CORYTHOSAURUS

Courtesy Department of Library Services, American Museum of Natural History: Neg. no. 37243, 53tl; Neg. no. 18502, 53ml; Neg. no. 18547, 54m; Neg. no. 18552, 54br, 55bl; Neg. no. 19488, 55tr; Neg. no. 19493, 55mr. Sternberg files, M. Walker Collection; University Archives/ Forsyth Library; Fort Hays State University, Hays, Kansas: 54ml, 55tl. Bruce Coleman/Mark N. Boulton: 63mr. Bridgeman Art Library: 63br.

Model photography by Dave King: 1br, 1bm, 3tl, 4br, 48-51, 58-59, 61b, 64–67, 68b,71br, 93tl.

Museum photography by Lynton Gardiner: 52bl, 55br, 56–57, 60b, 62tr, 63tl, 65bl, 65br, 68mr.

Additional special photography by Paul Bricknell (magnifying glass): 53tr; Andy Crawford: (children) 56tr, 56bl, 57tr, 57br, 68b.

### TRICERATOPS

Courtesy Department of Library Services, American Museum of Natural History: Neg. no. 18541, 74b; Neg. no. 18375, 76tl; Neg. no. 253875, 84tr; Neg. no. 251518, 84ml; Neg. no. 411955, 84bl; Neg. no. 410764, 84br; AMNH/Fred Conrad: 84. Sternberg files, M. Walker Collection; University Archives/ Forsyth Library; Fort Hays State

University, Hays, Kansas: 76ml, 76br, 77tl, 77ml, 77mr, 77br. Permission of the National Museum of Canada, Ottawa: 76mr. Bruce Coleman/RIM Campbell: 83br.

Model photography by Dave King: 1tr, 1m, 3bm, 4tr, 70, 71tl, 71bl, 72b, 73bl, 78-79m, 79tm, 80-81, 82–83, 90b 95b.

Museum photography by Lynton Gardiner: 75tl, 78–79b, 79tr, 86-87t, 87bl, 87r, 88-89, 90mr.

Additional special photography by Paul Bricknell: (magnifying glass) 75tr, 84mr; Andy Crawford: (children) 78bl, 90b; (model) 71r, 82tr; Jerry Young: 87m.

DK Publishing would like to thank Katherine Rogers for her help in researching images from the Sternberg files at the Forsyth Library, Fort Hays State University, Hays, Kansas. Roger Priddy for art directing photography at the American Museum of Natural History, and Rowena Alsey, Jonathan Buckley, Mandy Earey, and Sharon Peters for their help in producing this book.

Jacket: model photography by Dave King.

Thanks also to Andrew Abello, Darren Chin, Natalie Ebrey, Jennie Joannides, Katy King, Daniel Ray, and Jamie Ross, for appearing in this book.

Index by Lynn Bresler.